ANGELA THOMAS

WHEN WALLFLOWERS
dance

Becoming a Woman of **Righteous Confidence**

Published by

THOMAS NELSON

Since 1798

www.thomasnelson.com

Published in Nashville, Tennessee, by Thomas Nelson, Inc.

Published in association with Nelson Books and Creative Trust, Inc., Literary Division, 2105 Elliston Place, Nashville, TN 37203.

Thomas Nelson titles may be purchased in bulk for educational, business, fund-raising, or sales promotional use. For information, please e-mail SpecialMarkets@ThomasNelson.com.

Scripture quotations noted NKJV are taken from THE NEW KING JAMES VERSION. Copyright © 1979, 1980, 1982, Thomas Nelson, Inc., Publishers.

Scripture quotations noted NIV are from the HOLY BIBLE: NEW INTERNATIONAL VERSION®. Copyright © 1973, 1978, 1984 by International Bible Society. Used by permission of Zondervan Publishing House. All rights reserved.

Scripture quotations noted THE MESSAGE are from *The Message: The New Testament in Contemporary English.* Copyright © 1993 by Eugene H. Peterson.

Scripture quotations marked NCV are taken from the New Century Version®. Copyright © 1987, 1988, 1991 by Word Publishing, a division of Thomas Nelson, Inc. Used by permission. All rights reserved.

Library of Congress Cataloging-in-Publication Data

Thomas, Angela, 1962–
    When wallflowers dance : becoming a woman of righteous confidence /
Angela Thomas.
        p. cm.
    Includes bibliographical references.
    ISBN 10: 0-7852-6358-6 (hardcover)
    ISBN 10: 0-7852-8862-7 (tradepaper)
    ISBN 13: 978-0-7852-8862-6 (tradepaper)

    1. Christian women—Religious life. 2. Self-confidence—Religious aspects—Christianity. I. Title.
BV4527.T4688 2005
248.8'43—dc22   2005020844

Printed in the United States of America
07 08 09 10 11 RRD 5 4 3 2 1

For
Creative Trust

When I was just a wallflower,
you believed I could dance.

I love you all.

contents

There is . . . a time to dance.
—Ecclesiastes 3:1, 4 NKJV

foreword

As a professional counselor and life coach, I have encountered so many women over the years who fit the description of the un-woman in chapter one, including Angela. When I first met her several years ago, she was not empowered or confident. She could not make a stand and wasn't ready to champion her life the way God instructs women to in Scripture. The woman you read about in chapter one is the woman who came into my office underneath her circumstances and completely shut down . . . a wallflower.

Anyone who has seen or heard the remarkable testimony of this beautiful, dynamic, and intuitively wise speaker would never imagine in a million years that she is the same person who could relate to all those un-woman feelings of despair and hopelessness. But Angela is one of those rare modern-day Abigails we read about in 1 Samuel 25. She has sought the Lord, and because of her desire for God, she has overcome.

I have personally watched a miracle take place before my very own eyes. The wallflower is gone, and Angela is dancing. She is a strong voice who speaks from her deep pursuit of God. Because of Christ in her, women across the globe can hear a message of hope and victory through freedom in Christ. This next generation of women is blessed to have a light to illuminate their journeys. And the torch is carried by a woman who is more than a survivor; she is a hero.

I expect that you will have a fresh encounter with God through Angela's words. Take the time to learn from her. I wholeheartedly commend her message. I trust her heart. If there is anyone who can teach you how to dance, it's Angela.

—*Brian Irwin*
New Beginnings Coaching & Counseling
Knoxville, Tennessee

wall·flow·er (n)—*a shy or retiring person who remains unnoticed at social events, especially a woman without a dance partner (informal)* [1]

WORD HISTORY: The sweet-smelling flowers of *Cheiranthus cheiri* came to be called *wallflowers* because they often grow on old walls, rocks, and quarries. The plant name was first recorded in 1578. It is not known who first made the comparison between these delicate flowers and the unpartnered women sitting along the wall at a dance, but the figurative sense is first found in an 1820 work by Mrs. Campbell Praed entitled *County Ball.* Although originally used to describe women at dances, the word is now applied to men as well and used in situations remote from a ballroom. [2]

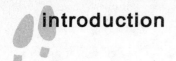

A Wallflower Gospel

My dear friend,

In my awkward high school years, I was the textbook wallflower in glasses and braces. Not too ugly. A little nerdy. Smart and active. But unknown. Present and observing, but seemingly transparent to others. No votes for homecoming court. No dates. And—especially painful back then—no one to ask me to dance.

I don't think that people meant not to see me. No one was rude to me or bullied me. It's just that they forgot to call. Forgot that I was funny. Forgot that I'd like to be invited to their parties too. In high school, I was very academic and busy with activities, but it felt as though I was in my own little world. My life was separate from others. It seemed other girls were noticed because they were beautiful or athletic or brilliant. I was typically unnoticed, and unnoticed seemed normal to me. So I just muddled through each day, and mostly they were very regular, extremely ordinary, fairly happy wallflower days that turned into wallflower years.

As I became a woman, the physical wallflower attributes began to fade, but the wallflower spirit was never too far away. In every little defeat or big discouragement, I'd find myself retreating into the heartache of being unseen and unknown. Eventually, it seemed wallflower was the role I was destined to play in some way through every season in my life. As it turns out, the woman who retreats into the spirit of wallflower eventually becomes an un-woman. Empty. Numb. Barely present. Just breathing and smiling and blending in to stay out of the way.

From my earliest memories, I have known of God and believed in the reality of His existence. But one day, right in the middle of my wallflower years, that truth became mine. I called God my Father and earnestly claimed Jesus as my Savior. As purely as I knew how, I wanted to return God's love with my life. But mine was a wallflower life, and I assumed it would continue to be that way with God. Mostly unseen and uneventful.

I knew that my name was written in God's Book of Life. I was assured of heaven and assumed that was as good as it gets. The wallflower woman who's just happy to be in the same room as God and very thankful to spend eternity in His heaven. Maybe if I stayed out of trouble and didn't call too much attention to my life, God would be pleased and He'd listen to my prayers, and that would be a good life to have.

Many of you know that my ordinary little life blew apart in divorce. Wallflowers aren't used to causing so much commotion. So I did the very thing I've always done to avoid pain. Hide. Blend. Smile anyway. Keep everyone out. Especially God.

But our God is a pursuing God. All those years as a believer, but I had never really known that about Him. Interesting that half my life had to go by so that I could get it. God came to find me. Really. He dragged me out of the dark and into the light. He held me close and gave me safety. As I came to know these deeper truths of His desire and passion for me, the most beautiful picture I could paint of His love was the very emotional picture of a wallflower being asked to dance.

This book is about dancing. There is the life you live with God, and there is the life you live when you are dancing in His arms. Dancing is living in the fullness of your purpose for this life on earth. Dancing is loving every single person God brings to you with the love He has so abundantly given. Dancing means you have eyes that can see what matters for eternity. Dancing is a passionate life. Adventure. And living without fear.

I believe that learning to dance in the arms of God requires total surrender to His sovereign will and a complete trust in His tender love. I have met women who just spend their lives with God. I have been that same kind of a woman many years of my life. But the woman who is dancing with God is fascinating. I want to be fascinating.

The difference between just living and dancing is spiritual maturity. Most of us don't know how to dance on our own; someone has to come along and show us how. For some reason, we believed that acquiring knowledge would get us there, but we've done that, and mostly we're smarter but not dancing. We hoped marriage would mean dancing until we learned that no one can give you what God intended to give you Himself. We prayed to just wake up one day dancing, a mature, brilliant, godly woman. But dancing is chosen.

God says to the woman He loves, "Would you like to?" And the woman responds with her life.

There is an old-fashioned term called *discipleship*. I asked my computer to define the word and it said, "No results were found." Very unfashionable. Not hip or cool. Not even in my cyber-dictionary. Some of my friends asked, "Should you tell people this book is about discipleship? That outdated term might turn some women off." And yet, there is no other way to grow in spiritual maturity apart from discipleship. To be discipled means that one is trained over an extended time. This kind of life training involves modeling, practicing, repetition, heart-to-heart honesty, and life application until the principles have been transferred from the teacher into the life of the learner. Jesus said that *the student who is fully trained will be like the teacher* (Luke 6:40). If our desire is to be like Jesus, then getting there means a training we have long called discipleship.

I believe that learning to dance with God requires intentional discipling. Waking up to your life is a process. Believing God, more than anything, is modeled and caught. Becoming a dancer requires lessons. Step-by-step. One foot in front of the other. A woman learning to feel and trust the rhythm of God's music for her life.

I took a whole course on discipleship in seminary. We spent an entire semester studying the principles Jesus used to train twelve men. And those men discipled others. And you and I will become captivating women, dancing in the arms of God, because of the power of discipleship to transform our lives. Women who have been discipled grow up. They learn how to hear the voice of their

Father. They understand how to respond to His grace. And they dance. Maybe timidly at first, but confidently in time.

Here is the good news of the wallflower gospel. God is coming across heaven and earth for you. Maybe you have already met Him. Maybe you are just beginning to hear His voice and recognize His glorious presence in your ordinary life. Either way, He is already here. Already pursuing your heart. Inviting you to step away from the edge of your life and into the center of His passion. Ready to give you a righteous confidence.

Righteous confidence comes from an abiding, deep assurance of God's presence in your life. Being sure of His unwavering interest in your heart and your family and your endeavors. Trusting that no matter what comes, God is for you. He goes ahead of you. He surrounds you with the fortress of His love. This kind of righteous confidence comes from spiritual maturity, and I like to think of spiritual maturity as dancing.

So my dear friend, no matter where life has you this day, lift up your weary head. Look into the eyes of your Father. Hear the music of His passionate love for you. When God is in the room, all the wallflowers get to dance.

Looking out from His arms,

—Angela
Spring 2005
Knoxville, Tennessee

AS I REFLECT on my own journey,
I become more and more aware of how
long I have played the role of observer . . .
I have never fully given up the role of
bystander. Even though there has been in
me a lifelong desire to be an insider looking out, I nevertheless kept choosing over
and over again the position of the outsider
looking in.

—*Henri Nouwen*[1]

CONSULT NOT YOUR fears but your
hopes and your dreams. Think not about
your frustrations, but about your unfulfilled
potential. Concern yourself not with what
you tried and failed in, but with what is still
possible for you to do.

—*Pope John XXIII*

chapter one

The Un-Woman

"Blueberries or strawberries?"

"Excuse me?"

"Which would you like, blueberries or strawberries?"

"I don't know. Whatever you think."

"It doesn't matter what I think. Choose what you like."

"I don't know what I like."

I was thirty-eight. A grown woman with half a lifetime of experiences. Fairly educated and organized. But I couldn't choose between blueberries or strawberries for dessert at a friend's dinner party. We laughed off my indecision, and I sat at the table watching my girlfriend serve me a little of both, wondering, *Why did that just cause me stress? Why don't I know what I like?* My silly quandary over dessert was just the beginning of a question that went home with me. In the next weeks, I kept turning those thoughts over and over in my mind. Eventually the deeper questions began to surface. *What kind of a woman is thirty-eight years old and doesn't know what she wants for dessert? Why don't I care about little things? Where did I go? Why don't I feel anything anymore? Why don't I enjoy anything? When did I stop becoming?*

It wasn't just that I couldn't make a decision about dessert; I began to realize that I really didn't know anything about me at all. I had no preferences. No top fives. No particular likes or dislikes. I had no idea what kind of music I liked to listen to, so mostly I listened to nothing. I couldn't tell you what my favorite restaurant was or if I'd like to go to the mountains or the beach for vacation. I couldn't choose a paint color with any confidence that I'd like it next week. I collected nothing for fear of collecting something I'd hate later. I realized I always chose what I thought would make someone else happy. About fifteen years of doing that and there was no me left.

I hadn't always been so uncommitted and uninteresting. I literally wore out an eight-track because I loved the funky music of Earth, Wind & Fire in high school. I was adamant about wanting yellow shag carpeting with daisy light fixtures in my bedroom. Mama's fried cube steak was my favorite food, and cherry pie was my favorite dessert. I read everything Lois Lenski ever wrote. I wanted to be the best varsity cheerleader in our county. I loved waking up and I loved Jesus and my youth group and a cherry cola called Cheerwine. I remember laughing a lot back then. And I remember the *Angela* I was discovering inside me.

College and seminary were vibrant years that I can play back in my head in Technicolor. The world was alive to me. God was my passion. I could see and touch and feel. It seems I danced a lot back then. And told jokes. And trusted God. Still excited and still hoping.

But about four years ago, I was a grown woman in a daze. I kind of knew I was dead to life because I could see other people living out there somewhere, but I didn't believe I could ever be alive again. Actually, I'm not sure I even wanted a real life with real passion. I had become the un-person. Neutral. Safe. Asleep. Numb. Vanilla. Harmless. With an un-life. Going through the motions. Surviving. Reacting. Smiling. Somewhere along the way, I had given up. I guess somewhere along the way, it seemed the easiest thing to do.

My Un-Becoming

Most of us don't just wake up one morning and think to ourselves, *I am officially giving up on life. I am checking out. Numbing down. Going nowhere. Only breathing and surviving from here on out.* But for many of us it happens anyway. Various degrees of giving up. Various degrees of an un-person with an un-life.

I have tried to retrace my steps to figure out what happened to the woman I was becoming all those years ago.

I have a firstborn, pleaser personality. Born to Joe and Novie in Mt. Airy, North Carolina, I am the oldest child with two younger brothers and a sister in heaven. My sister died when she was two, so most of my life, I have been the firstborn, only daughter. I always knew being the only girl in the house was pretty special. I was twelve when my sister, Amanda, was born and fourteen when she died. After she was gone, I took the responsibility of being the only daughter even more seriously.

Our childhood was stable and very good. Hard work was valued and modeled and applauded. Being lazy or grumbling or playing around wasn't tolerated. Being honest and funny was highly treasured. We had vacations at the beach, family reunions, and afternoons in the mountains. There was always plenty to eat. And we went to church every Sunday because we had no idea that attendance was optional.

All in all, it was a ho-hum, very ordinary, do-your-homework, sheltered-little-girl kind of life. My parents didn't care what anyone else thought or what the latest fashions were or where other people went or what music they listened to. My mom made almost all of my clothes. We ate tomato sandwiches instead of going to McDonald's. My only teenage job was at my dad's produce stand on the side of the road, learning the fine art of sorting rotten potatoes, bagging Christmas candy, and being nice to people. Possibly, everything I needed to know about interacting with the world, I learned selling produce. If I could sum it all up in one sentence, I think those years taught me to be nice every chance I get because people are really hurting.

Ho-hum and ordinary don't mean perfect. My family is weird and dysfunctional in our own quirky ways. We don't show our anger or frustration. That is weird, and a lifetime of no perceived anger has to be wrong somehow. But there is an exception to the rule. In the event that someone you love is being hurt or violated, then it's okay to be angry. We act happy all the time even when we're not. Not many exceptions to that one. We quickly stuff our hurts and don't bring them up again. Time better heal because we're not going to talk about it. We ride in the car a lot. No kidding. Very weird family trait. We don't put together puzzles or play board games; we all cram into the car and ride around. We laugh about "riding around" now, but we all still do it. When I don't know what else to do, I put the kids in the car and ride until we find it. I'm sure there are many other dysfunctional attributes of our family that are highly visible to the rest of the world, but I've stuffed them so far down, they're difficult to retrieve at the moment.

I was raised naive and insulated. I don't know if that's the best way, but it's all I knew. I trusted everybody, loved with all my heart, and assumed my personal mission was to bring joy and happiness to the world, or at least to the folks who came to the produce stand. At some point, I realized that I got a lot of energy from making everyone else happy. So keeping people happy eventually became more important than knowing my purpose or becoming anything. I would stand on my head to make people happy. Spin plates or juggle flaming swords. Anything to get some kind of affirming response.

Guess what I found out? You can never really make anybody happy. They decide in their own little hearts if they will pursue a lifetime of peace and cultivate a joyful spirit. Takes a long time to learn that. Spinning plates takes its toll. Trying to catch flaming swords ends up burning and wounding. A big part of me went away through the years in the effort to please.

As a mom, having four children in seven years took its toll on my heart. I thought I could be the most amazing mother on the planet, but it turns out that survival was about the best I could do. They were clean and fed, but my soul fell fast asleep in those baby years. I didn't mean for it to happen. I tried to pretend it didn't, but a little of me died in the ten years of diapers.

I was married fourteen years. The divorce was embarrassing. In all those years my heart grew numb in order to cope. More of me was gone.

One day my brother said to me, "I haven't seen my sister in thirteen years. She just went away, and I don't recognize who you've become." I hurt over his words, but I knew they were true. I knew that I was gone; I just didn't realize that anyone else missed me.

Add up the years and the events. My ridiculous need to please. The people and the pain. The weariness of an overwhelming life. Take away the community that comes from honesty. Take away the spiritual nourishment that could have come from being known and understood. Add the pride of a woman who refuses to own her flaws or admit to her wounds. Stir in fear. Worry. Doubt. Insecurity. The lies we come to believe. Subtract vulnerability. Heap on pretending. There you have the woman I was becoming.

The un-woman just trying to blend in. Giving up a little more every day. The one who couldn't even choose between berries. A woman just watching the world go by. Afraid. Without confidence. A wallflower.

The Wallflowers Among Us

As it turns out, I am not the only woman to ever give up and retreat into the barren life of a wallflower. I recognize that familiar emptiness in women everywhere I go. I sit beside women on airplanes. I look into their eyes at conferences. I live in their neighborhood and go to church with them and wait in carpool lines with women who are going away. Playing it safe. Blending in. Unbecoming. I can look around my life right now and count the women close to me who are somewhere in the process of giving up on living.

Believe me, I get it. Depending on your circumstances, it can feel like the most painless option to give in to nothingness or lose yourself in the chaos of busyness. I became the un-woman in an effort to avoid the relationship land mines all around me. Like that worked. Then there was some weird decision that I didn't deserve anything more than a numb, timid existence. And then sometimes it even seemed the more spiritual thing to emotionally fade to gray. Be quiet. Remain unseen and unknown. Forget about becoming anything. Neutral. Unrecognizable.

More and more, it seems so many women are surviving decades of their lives by turning their hearts inside out, trying not to feel. Becoming the un-woman.

The Years Go By

Marriage is hard. No married person I've ever met would disagree. Several people I know are in very difficult marriages and remain there because it's the right thing to do. I believe that apart from abuse, staying is the right thing. But as these women stay, I'm also watching them fade to nothing, emotionally going under because the relationship is so bad. I was married and now I'm not, so I probably don't have the right to say anything except that maybe I can see even more clearly from this side. I can see the woman I used to be, and I can see that people might try if they could feel again. It's just that most of us are putting more effort into trying not to feel. And blaming the other person. And counting up short-comings. And all around us, married women are un-becoming. After a while, the two who used to love each other can come to believe that the pain would go away if the marriage did. The divorced among us know that the pain remains.

I know moms who wake up every morning and go through the motions with their kids, but the heart of mothering is passing them by. Disappointment and responsibility have taken their toll. So they complain about schedules instead of sketching out their dreams. Being the snack mom for soccer this week might just push their fragile hearts over the edge. Moms are tired, and the whole parenting gig is not anything like they thought it was going to be, so they send snippy e-mails about their kid being excluded from an overnight and start little rumors about the teachers because it's just about all they can control.

Then there's the mom with the teenager who barely speaks to her anymore. It's too much to feel that kind of rejection from someone you love so much. So the mom goes away on the inside and smiles on the outside and keeps thinking of something to make for dinner. And the babies become lacrosse players while she is unbecoming.

I talk to a lot of single women and single moms and teenage girls who don't feel anything anymore. They tell me about their pain because they think that I might understand. Unfortunately, I am well acquainted with their loneliness. A desperate, quiet ache that suffocates joy. A private emotional drowning. An unseen heart in an unseen place with unseen pain. We get tired of talking about it because, really, things could be so much worse. What does lonely matter—compared to having a terminal disease or homelessness? So we try not to complain and we act like we're brave. One time I heard someone say, "Embrace your loneliness and let it work for you." That's one of the all-time dumbest things I've ever heard. Lonely, unnoticed people become the un-people. Wallflowers who wish someone would ask them to dance.

Sometimes It's All Too Much

What is it with our society and the pressure to perform, the ridiculous demands, the injury of selfishness, and the incredible pain? Almost every person I know has more heartache and responsibility than any one person should have to bear.

A few weeks ago I was crying on the phone to my girlfriend. Poor thing. She's a couple of thousand miles away. We've known each other almost twenty years, and we talk about once a week. Every so often, usually around midnight when I'm using my last ounce of rational, balanced, thinking person to drive home from the airport, I make her feel completely helpless by falling apart on the phone. My girlfriend will be three time zones away listening to my run-on sentences, trying to make out what I'm saying in between the tears, wiping my nose, and squinting my way home in the dark.

Not so long ago during one of those late-night episodes, I was rattling off the list of my responsibilities. Feeling that I was crumbling underneath the pressure to perform. She let me ramble for a while and then said, "Ang, it's just too much. You have more to carry than one person should have." I know it sounds crazy, but somehow that made me feel better. *Yeah*, I realized, *this is too much. No one should have to carry the whole thing by herself. It's okay to cry and babble. No wonder people just go to nothing. Sometimes it's all too much.*

I know that I am covered up with commitments, requests, children, financial obligations, and more pressure than I know what to do with. And I don't have a marriage relationship to figure out! With all I've got going on, I can only imagine the unending demands and stress that some women face. It's too much. In the effort to oblige and perform for everyone else, the heart suffers. The soul is emptied. The mind goes numb. And we just want to get through this day as best we can, without feeling.

Trying Not to Feel

I understand why no one wants to feel. In my most devastating season of separation, the children and I were living with my parents. I was crying endlessly. My body began to respond to my heartache with hair loss and twitching eyes. I experienced anxiety attacks, shortness of breath, and nausea. I was a scary, emotional mess. My parents feared I was right at the edge of a mental ward (and I was) and sent me to their family doctor. I left with a prescription for an antidepressant, a drug that would reduce the intensity of my feeling. I held on to that paper for almost a year.

The prescription stayed in my purse unfilled, because for six months I didn't have to function. I was a stay-at-home mom and during that time, my only activity every day was to take the children back and forth to school. Then I would crawl back into bed downstairs at my parents' house, cry, and sleep for the rest of the day. In all those months, my mom fed us and kept the laundry clean until I could find my way back. I cannot imagine what it would have been like if I had needed to get dressed for work at an office, show up responsible, make decisions, and then go home to care for a family. The pain was too great. I'm sure I would have filled every prescription the doctor would have given to me.

Almost every person I know has at some point been written a prescription that will help him or her keep from feeling. I get it. There are wayward children, distant husbands, empty retirement funds, more bills than money, terrorists, and dread diseases. Life is very hard. It can become too much to feel it all at once.

Women hole up in their homes hoping the world will go away because the world has already caused them so much hurt. It has stolen their hope. Not much happens as you'd dreamed, and things have already turned out crummy, so what's the use anyway? We back away from honest relationships because people hurt us. They tell others your struggles. They respond with legalism. They draw circles that keep you out. All over the world, people are choosing cyber relationships over the real thing and cyber love and the illusions of cyber reality. Becoming invisible. Interacting without feeling. Minimizing the potential for pain.

You'd think that women would be flocking to church. The place where they should be able to receive help. The one place with answers. But sadly, the very place that could offer the greatest healing has hurt so many with bad counsel or destructive labeling. The stories could fill pages. There was a woman whose husband had been fired from two jobs because he had been the proven perpetrator in sexual harassment cases. She caught him having yet another affair. She went to the church, but they told her she needed more proof of his philandering. They counseled her to stay with him. He got another woman pregnant. She left the church devastated by their lack of concern for her protection.

Another woman privately shared her struggle with an eating disorder and asked for prayer. In about a week, she was asked to step down from her nursery rotation to give her time to "deal with her issues." The one thing that gave her joy, caring for the three-year-olds, was taken away in the one place she could have been given hope.

Defeated on so many fronts, women are tired of trying. They are present but just watching. Observers. Wallflowers.

Sandy has been a widow for eight years. Her three children are teenagers, and they barely get by financially. Sandy is smart and savvy, but never finished college even though she says she'd like to. She works part-time in the returns department at a local home improvement store. Years have gone by and many friends and family members have given her every encouragement to go back to school. They've offered money and help with the children. They can see her potential. They can see that she is strong and organized and hardworking. Sandy's friends see that she was made for dancing, but recognize that she's only watching. Sandy says she'll get there one day, and maybe she will. But the years race past and it seems she's afraid of something better. Like she's afraid to improve or learn. Like being a wallflower is safe and dancing is dangerous.

A while ago I had a very specific conversation with a woman. Her children were grown. The house was clean enough. She had the whole rest of her life to live. "What do you love?" I asked. "What are your passions? If you could dream big or become anything, what would it be? Let's pray together, hear from God, get a plan, and work the plan." She was enthusiastic and at the time seemed motivated to go forward. We talked about it a few more times over the next months. At least three years have gone by since our first conversation. The kids are a little older. The house is a little cleaner. She has prayed and prayed. Nothing has changed in her life or in her purpose. Wallflower is a safe place, and she is choosing to stay there. I think she's afraid of becoming.

I know what it feels like to be afraid. As many options as there are for fear, it seems one or many can get into my head and paralyze my heart. And when my heart is seized with fear, then I stand still or pull inside my emptiness to mourn. Then life goes by without me. And years go by without any significant growth or change.

Even worse, time can go by and a woman can emotionally begin to fade away. Barely noticeable at first. Only a little giving in to fear at a time. And then one day, the woman who has lived gripped by fear has watched it all pass by. There are no days left. She missed her purpose. Fear won, and the wallflower is all she's become.

There Is a Thief

There is a thief, and he comes to steal our becoming, kill our dreams, and destroy our very lives. He comes to make you an un-woman with an un-life. He wants to make you harmless and obscure. Through the years it seems I became afraid of all the things I thought I really wanted. Afraid of adventure. Afraid of love. Afraid of change.

A few months ago I asked 150 women to fill out a survey. These women had come to a conference I was teaching, and this particular group of women was a great representation of our diversity. There were women of every age and from every walk of life. Young moms. Single women. Teenage girls. Professional teachers, attorneys, and physicians. Women from the fashion and music industries. Several women retired with grandchildren. Some of them were very wealthy. Most were in between. And about a dozen women came that weekend from the rescue mission.

I had created the questionnaire specifically for this group of women. I wanted to take their pulse, look for the differences, and focus on our similarities. One of the questions asked was: Why aren't we becoming the women we've always wanted to be? The women were allowed to give as many answers as they could think of. Almost every woman listed fear in some way.

I began to ask myself, *What if we could diminish fear in the hearts of women? What if we began to live and respond from courage? What if fear lost its grip and the wallflowers began to step out of the shadows? What if women could begin to live in a righteous confidence?*

I get so excited about the ideas of passion and women living amazing lives. I can almost taste my desire to help women grow in their giftings and my desire to see them face their everyday lives with courage. But almost every time I begin to sound big and bold, my rah-rah words are met with a reluctant, you-can't-move-me smile from the person I'm talking to. I spent more than an hour yesterday talking to a woman who is a casual acquaintance at the gym. She'll be fifty-two on Saturday. The conversation began innocently enough.

"What are you doing for your birthday?" I asked in between crunches.

"Oh, probably nothing. Maybe we'll go out to dinner the night before. I really need to work in the yard that day. Anyway, I'm over having birthdays. What's the big deal? It almost seems like they come twice a year now. We don't like to spend money, and I don't like the idea of being fifty-two. Besides, I partied plenty when I was younger."

"I'm not talking about partying. I'm talking about a celebration. Look at your life. You are healthy. You have a job you like. Your husband loves you. Another year has gone by and you shouldn't miss celebrating all you've been given. Get the people you love together and whoop it up."

"I don't like being with the people I love. They get on my nerves."

"Then get some people you like together."

"I don't want to."

"You can afford to get on a plane and go to New York for a weekend. Have a fabulous dinner and see a show."

"Don't want to."

"Why are you afraid to enjoy being alive?"

"I'm not afraid, I just don't care anymore. I'm over it."

My friend really is over it. She stopped taking vacations about five years ago. She and her husband don't exchange gifts anymore. *It's a waste of money.* She goes back and forth to work. Takes her husband for granted. Lives for her dogs. Watches her favorite programs on television. Takes her mom to lunch on Sundays. Counts her carbs. Surfs the Internet. Hides in the routine. The thief has numbed down her life, and he has won.

She could have thirty amazing years in front of her or she could have just two. But either way, she's going to miss them. My friend is loud and dominant and very opinionated, all from the safety of her insulated, fenced-in world. She has been hurt through the years.

My friend's business failed several years ago, so she's mad at the federal government about taxes and the city government about zoning restrictions and anyone else she can think of to blame. She used to play lead guitar in a rock band, but she doesn't play anymore because the band never got picked up by a recording label and she's still huffy about it. Even though she's been married twenty-seven years, she and her husband never had any children because it just never seemed to be the right time. Her marriage is committed, but boring by her and her husband's own admission.

Life disappointments and personal, private hurts have all just piled together for her. She had some failures, but they have become her focus. You begin to believe what you focus on, and now she is living as if she is a failure. And from her self-imposed protection, she doesn't do anything or interact with anyone that could possibly bring her pain again. She's so afraid over there in her sterilized, numbed-down world. Perpetually disappointed. Not really living.

She is just one of us. One who more openly displays her fear. But there are many more of us who live from the same kind of fear, except with a little more pretending. We're over it on the inside. Life holds no fascination. Adventure sounds exhausting. Friendships aren't worth it. We're tired, and we want to be left alone. Being a wallflower sounds like that long nap we've been needing.

- Are you tired? I imagine that you are because everyone I know is exhausted.
- Are you disappointed, depressed, or even worse, hopeless? You are not alone.

- Have your dreams all died or maybe you have failed
  in their pursuit?
- Have you become afraid of everything or a lot
  of things?

Or maybe your want-to is just plain wearing out and you feel like my forty-three-year-old girlfriend, who told me she thinks she's done enough. She's tired and empty, and she says she'll be ready to die at fifty.

I hear you and some days I'm with you, but you cannot give up. Evidently, you woke up this morning still breathing. And every day you are left on this earth is a day that God intended for your life to matter. Not only does your life matter, I do not believe that God means for any of us to live an un-person, un-life, wallflower existence. I believe He meant for us to dance.

Groove On

When was the last time you danced?

The last time I got dressed up and went to a place where there was dancing was about fifteen years ago. Let me just say right off the bat, that is ridiculously too long ago. I was seven months pregnant with my first baby. We had gone to a wedding where there was dancing at the reception. I'm sure I looked goofy out on the dance floor with a big shrouded tummy, but I don't remember caring. And it didn't seem anyone else cared either. We all just danced. Except for a couple I didn't know, who stood over in the corner and smiled. I heard that they didn't think Jesus would want them to dance at a wedding reception.

Maybe we don't think Jesus wants us to dance either. Too frivolous. Too happy. Something awful could happen, and we might get carried away and start dancing every day. Maybe we have forgotten that the man after God's heart danced.

> *Then David danced with all his might before the* LORD.
>
> (2 Samuel 6:14 NCV)

I grew up in the Methodist Church, so I'm thankful that I'd never once heard of the no-dancing rule until I met some people in seminary who didn't dance for Jesus either. I was so glad I hadn't known that rule earlier in my life. That would have totally ruined four years of college dancing. By the time I heard about the no-dancing policy, I was old enough to realize that it was possibly one of the most profoundly absurd, life-killing, stick-in-the-mud rules anybody ever made up.

Why do we always go to extremes? Not one time in all my years of formals, cheerleading, and goof-off dancing at home did it ever occur to me to jump up on a table and act lewd. Course that's how many teenagers dance now, but that's not the dancing I'm talking about.

Here's what I mean. I don't get invited to very many places where there is formal, dress-up dancing, but in our family, we dance anyway. In our house when one of the kids does anything worth a little yahoo, I say to them, "Up high," and they give me a high five.

"Down low," and there's a low five.

"Groove on," and we both do some silly dance. A few nights ago I was sitting on the side of William's bed for our nightly unwinding time in the dark. He is eight years old, and we were talking about the day. William remembered to tell me about a compliment the teacher had given him that day. I think it was for walking in a straight line on the way to lunch. "Up high," I said, and he found my hand in the dark.

"Down low," and again he gave me five.

"Groove on," and both of his sleepy arms came out from under the covers for a wiggly-little-lying-down dance in the dark.

In our family, we dance for celebration and we dance for fun and we dance because it makes us laugh and feel alive. I am absolutely sure that God wants you to dance the dance of your life in His arms.

Shall We Dance?

Several years ago I came to understand that I am held by the lavish, never-ending love of God. That kind of love means there are no women relegated to wallflower lives. Day to day is very difficult for most of us, but we do not have to become the un-woman with the un-life. We do not have to numb down and go away. God intended so much more. The woman who belongs to God gets to dance. Inside the strength of His embrace, you can become the woman you have always wanted to be . . . the one He dreamed of when He dreamed of you.

The next chapters are about learning to dance. Really starting to live, no matter where you are or the circumstances you face. We're going to talk about becoming a grown-up, confident woman, young or old, who runs toward maturity and strength. We are going to claim the promises of God. We are going to hear and respond to His plans. Too many of us have already gone away. But none of us have to stay there.

Dancing requires a little courage. Enough confidence to get out there and try. Enough chutzpah to move to the music or take a few lessons.

Maybe your soul is sleepy. Maybe your heart aches underneath all the burdens you carry. Maybe you have given up on ever becoming the woman you used to dream of being. Maybe thinking about dancing makes you tired. Stay with me.

This day I want you to hear the truth. Your Creator has amazing plans that still lie in front of you. No matter what has come to you, the disappointments you have known, the consequences you have received, or the wounds that have kept you down. Even if you have truly failed or wasted a lot of precious time. Hear me shout this life-giving truth:

It is never too late to dance with God!

He'll take your threadbare dreams and weave a tapestry called your purpose. He'll plow a brand-new road to lead you out of the lost place you've ended up.

God looks across the room at the un-woman who is giving up and fading away, the woman He has never stopped loving, and He asks that wallflower to dance.

Jesus said, *I came to give life—life in all its fullness* (John 10:10 NCV), and no woman who makes her life in Christ has to live empty.

So altogether now, up high.

Down low.

Groove on.

a dancing lesson

Sometimes it's just one foot in
front of the other. Throw your
feet over the side of the bed.
Strap on the shoes that
make you feel pretty. And
decide to move in the
direction of the woman
you've always wanted
to become.

I HAVE BEEN led to an inner place where I had not been before. It is the place within me where God has chosen to dwell. It is the place where I am held safe in the embrace of an all-loving Father who calls me by name and says, "You are my beloved, on you my favor rests." It is the place where I can taste the joy and the peace that are not of this world.

—*Henri Nouwen*[1]

I AM A FRIEND of God. He calls me friend.

—*Michael Gungor and Israel Houghton*

THOSE WHO CRY as they plant crops will sing at harvest time.

—*Psalm 126:5* NCV

 **chapter two**

Before You Give Up

I f I could sit down and talk to you today, I'd choose a day like yesterday. Yesterday our church had its big anniversary celebration outside under a tent. After the worship service, there were lunch for eight hundred and a fall festival for the kids. I had the privilege of pulling up a hay bale beside a woman who was just about to give up. The sun was shining. We each were balancing a plateful of sloppy barbecue with baked beans and coleslaw on our knees. I had all the time in the world while the kids played, and I was very grateful she asked me to listen.

Her story was a lot like the one I have lived. Divorced, single mom. Grieving and wondering how in the world she is ever going to make it. Lonely. Becoming bitter. Afraid and believing that she is all alone in the dark. I'm not sure I had anything powerful to give her that day except the testimony of being a few years down the road and truly coming to know a very beautiful life, in spite of all that's happened. Sometimes just talking to someone who's making it can keep you from giving up.

Lord knows that every time I am just about to give up, some

caring person in my life has pulled up a chair or gotten on a plane or driven through the night to talk me back. One of the most memorable conversations I've ever had was about five years ago. I was in the middle of my separation and desperately searching for answers. The whole thing was so personally embarrassing and humbling. I just wanted to move into a cave or, better yet, evaporate. Anything but face all that was in front of me.

One afternoon, I was at home all by myself where I had been crying off and on most of the morning. That day seemed unbearable, and thinking about the future felt even more dark and hopeless. I was truly at one of the lowest points I had ever known—fully operating as an un-woman with an un-life. I couldn't hear God or feel His love. I couldn't see the next step, and I feared any step would only multiply the pain. I had no earthly idea what to do next. Worn out from the crying, I had lain down on my bed for a nap, and as my tears were turning into sleep, I said to God, "I am so lost. I can't feel. I can't think. Will You please just call me on the phone and tell me what to do?"

An hour later I woke up to the phone ringing. It was Dennis, my friend who is a pastor in California. I interned for Dennis when I was in seminary, and we have been friends ever since. After my graduation, we had kept in touch a few times a year. Dennis called to check in that day with no idea what he was getting ready to hear.

He finally heard the truth I had been hiding. It was ugly and awkward to tell the man who had poured so much into me about the path my life had taken. We talked for more than an hour. He asked very particular questions, and I sat on the floor beside my bed, exhausted from the retelling. Empty. Sad. I remember sitting there feeling disengaged and hopeless. I had disappointed yet another person in my life. How many more times would this have to happen? Then Dennis said to me, "Angela, listen to me. I am going to tell you exactly what to do."

Can you imagine what those words meant to me? I had just asked God to call me on the phone and tell me what to do. Then a spiritual mentor I haven't talked to in months calls me on the phone and says, "I'm going to tell you exactly what to do." I jumped to my feet and stood there fumbling for a pad of paper and a pen. God was answering my prayer right that minute, and I had to write it down.

Then Dennis began to gently give me step-by-step instructions. It was as if he were reaching through the phone line and across the country to stoop down and tenderly pick me up. I couldn't see a thing, I didn't have any idea what to do next, but his words spoke into my darkness and began to call me out. I believe God called me on the phone that day through Dennis. I believe He answered my prayer with a clarity I hadn't realized was possible. I believe God loves me so much that He came to rescue His beloved when she had lost her way.

Ever since that afternoon, I have talked to Dennis and his wife, Karen, at least once a week, sometimes more. He calls to "check my pulse" and plays a very huge role in my life as faithful mentor and consistent friend. A couple of months later I told Dennis about my prayer that day and how God had answered through him. He said, "Angela, I have never in my whole life told anyone, 'I am going to tell you exactly what to do.'" That's my God. My great, big God. I want you to know that He is your great, big God too.

> *Listen to the voice of the Father.*
>
> *He is saying, "You are My Beloved. My favor rests on you."*

May I Take You by the Hand?

Maybe you have lost your way. Maybe you've only been surviving the past few years. Or maybe you have become the un-woman with the un-life. I imagine that you've already tried a million things to overcome your emptiness. A fresh attitude. Getting up early to pray. A Bible study that might have the answer. A low-carb diet. The newest yoga class. A different church or a different job or a different husband. Maybe you've come to the end of your dreams and you refuse to try anything else—you've completely given up. Maybe you find yourself where I have been, sitting in the dark, despondent and desperate, praying that you'll just disappear.

Walking around on the earth is dangerous. Giving out your love can be painful. So many things come to us that steal our living. Disease, disappointment, busyness, consequences, circumstances, and failure. I understand why some moms begin drinking in secret to anesthetize their lives. I understand mind-numbing television watching or chick-lit novels or ridiculous shopping. Checking out can make a lot of sense in light of the heartache most women carry. The mind is screaming, *Get me out of here!* And it seems you can't get away from the pain.

I heard about a woman my age who parked her car on a train track one morning. The lights were flashing and the gate was coming down and she intentionally drove onto the center of the tracks and sat there, right in the path of the oncoming train. I imagine that she felt as if there was nowhere else to go and no way out, and her heart just wanted not to feel. None of us have to become so desperate. We can be sure of the hope that awaits us.

Sometimes, when we have become the un-woman with the un-life, not feeling seems the only way, and sitting alone in the dark seems to be all that we deserve. But the soul desperately knows it was made for more. One of my favorite authors, Henri Nouwen, wrote about the truth of our spiritual condition:

> *It often seems that the more I try to disentangle myself from the darkness, the darker it becomes. I need light, but that light has to conquer my darkness, and that I cannot bring about myself. I cannot forgive myself. I cannot make myself feel loved. By myself I cannot leave the land of my anger. I cannot bring myself home nor can I create communion on my own. I can desire it, hope for it, wait for it, yes, pray for it. But my true freedom I cannot fabricate for myself. That must be given to me. I am lost. I must be found and brought home by the shepherd who goes out to me.*[2]

Maybe you can't think anymore, your body is exhausted, and your heart has given up. Maybe you are weary of wandering through the years and tired of squinting through blurry vision. Maybe your soul has crawled into bed and cried itself to sleep. Maybe you need someone to come into your life, bend down to pick you up, and boldly say, "The Shepherd has found you. He is bringing you home. There will be dancing when you get there. Listen to me now. I am going to tell you exactly what to do."

With your permission, I want to take you by the hand and tenderly tell you what God has done for me so that you will know exactly what to do.

My Heart's Desire for You

God called me on the phone that day and dramatically, baby-step by baby-step, began to call me out. On the long journey since, He has continued revealing to me the deeper truths of His love and their application in my life. He has set me free from the bondage of un-woman and asked me to dance the dance of my life in His arms. If I could pull up a hay bale beside you today and look into your teary eyes, I would long to tell you everything I have learned coming out of the dark. You do not have to live like an un-woman with an un-life. This book contains the lessons I have learned on my way out of the dark.

It seems everywhere I go, I meet the coolest women who love God, but I also meet so many hurting, disappointed women who are just about to give up. These women have such an intense hunger, but many find themselves spiritually or emotionally stuck. The reasons we get bogged down are different for each of us, but I've come to see that the heart is so much the same. It longs for more. The heart longs for the life God dreamed of. For a deeper relationship with our Father. For greater discernment. Wisdom. Passion and adventure.

I believe that everything I've been through in the past years, even the desperate heartache, has been for the purpose of maturity, so that I would grow in wisdom and right living. I have not come into these truths because I am a sage, wise old bird. I think that I've tripped into almost every lesson God has taught to me. But if I can save you one more day of heartache and if God can use my clumsiness for His glory, then none of it will have been wasted.

More than anything, I want to be a mature follower of Christ. I am tired of the baby ways and the immature attitudes. I don't want to choose poorly or make decisions from emptiness. I want to grow up, really being transformed, because I am in a determined, dependent relationship with the Son of God, my Lord and Savior, Jesus Christ. Even in these years of mothering and providing, I want to step up to the personal and private challenge of becoming all that God intended.

So many of us desire to go to the next level with God, but we don't quite know how to get there. I used to teach a women's Bible study in Nashville. For about seven years, we met together on Tuesday nights, and I tried to teach the women what God had been teaching me. We spent a lot of years doing life together. Retreats. Breakfast meetings. Parties. Baby showers. I knew each of the women pretty well. We prayed together through tough decisions and loved one another through disappointments.

In seminary we called that kind of relationship *discipleship*: when one follower of Christ trains another follower in the truths he or she has learned.

I may not be able to look into your eyes, or call you on the phone, or meet with you on Tuesday nights, but in these pages it's my heart's desire to disciple you in the truths God has been teaching me. I want us to grow up together. I want you to go to the next place with God. In these chapters I will try to outline for you, as clearly as possible, the path God has used to bring me out of my un-life. It would be an honor to take you by the hand and walk beside you from the dark place into the light. From your un-life into your becoming. From fear into confidence.

I want to give to you what God gave to me that desperate afternoon when Dennis called. Just before you give up, I am asking God to tell you exactly what to do. I am pleading for Him to take all the lessons and all the pain, the Bible truths I have come to understand and the places where I am still in process, and use all of it or any part of it to lead you out. I am begging God to show you the way He wants you to go.

I want you to step up into the next level of knowing God. I want you to be amazed by His soul restoration and find rest in the security of His love. I want you to become the woman He always dreamed you would be. I want you to dance.

And So We Begin

I realize that when you are hurting or lost or overwhelmed, the last thing you really want to do is think or pray, but hang in there. I promise that God is going to make a way for you. Right now, your heart toward God might be numb, but I am going to believe enough for both of us. I know firsthand what He can do with women who don't think they can go on. I can't wait for you to watch our God turn your life around. I've seen Him do it over and over again in the lives of women all around me, and I am so grateful to be one of the many He will send to show you it can be true for you.

> *Central to the Christian experience is an unchanging belief that God is at work in all things for the good of those who love Him (Romans 8:28), and that means all things. He is particularly at work when we are stuck in pain that seems to be endless and meaningless.*[3]

As we begin, I am going to pray for you, but as you read along, would you agree with me in your heart before our Father? If you can, take a minute to slip to your knees or even lie facedown as you pray. Read this prayer out loud if you need to, so that you can pray it as your own. Do whatever is necessary to push away all the distraction for a few moments so that you can engage your heart as you pray.

> *Father God, I bring everything I am and everything I am not and I lay it down at Your feet. God, I want the life You dreamed of for me, but I am tired. I can't find my way. I have taken steps and fallen. I am without a hope of my own. I don't even feel worthy of such a life. So, God, come into my darkness and show me the way out. Please keep every promise You have made to me. Heal and restore my soul. Bend down and lift me up. Forgive me. Oh, Lord, please come and carry me to a higher place. In the name of Jesus, amen.*

We are beginning in prayer and we will move forward by prayer. I'm going to ask you to pray through every new teaching we come to. As a reminder, I don't know of anything powerful that happens in the human spirit apart from prayer. I realize that life may have you prayed out or bummed out right now, but press into this discipline even if you don't feel like it. Let your lack of want remind you of your great need.

> Be still and know the I-am-ness of God. Be quiet
> and hear the present now-ness of your Father.
> —Mark Pate

I have several friends who model for me the power of "praying anyway." My girlfriend Lynne prays through the darkness of chemotherapy and breast cancer, trusting even though she lacks clarity, and believing in God's strong presence even without answers. Another friend has prayed through the anger and rejection of discovering her husband's affair. Even though paralyzed with pain, she faithfully prayed through the months it took until she could get to true forgiveness and the decision to work toward restoration. There is a difference between "feeling" and praying anyway. We'll eventually get to the "feel like it," but the first thing that needs to happen is placing your heart in the presence of God through prayer.

So That Your Soul Can Catch Up

I am going to ask you to do what you are sure you cannot. I'm going to ask you to stop doing almost everything for a season. In many ways, the dark years forced me to lay down my commitments. In other ways, I didn't have the emotional energy to continue. But I can now see how pivotal a time of stopping has been for me. I felt that God led me to take two years off, and I believe that decision was foundational for the spiritual growth I have experienced.

Let me explain a little more. I have to provide for my family, so for those two years I did not stop working or caring for our daily needs. Maybe my life looked pretty normal from the outside. Three meals a day, folded laundry, keeping the bathrooms clean, mowing the yard, running the kids around, and traveling for work when the children were with their dad. But on the inside I realized that I needed to dial back from further commitments.

I had agreed to participate in some programs and committees, so I finished everything I had promised to do and then I stopped. Completely stopped. Even when prodded or guilted, I didn't budge. It took much too long to realize, but I couldn't avoid the obvious any longer—around the end of my thirties, my body had outrun my soul. Something dramatic had to change, or I was going to end up a little puddle of nothing.

In his book *Restoring Your Spiritual Passion*, Gordon MacDonald recounts a story by Lettie Cowman:

> In the deep jungles of Africa, a traveler was making a long trek. Coolies had been engaged from a tribe to carry the loads. The first day they marched rapidly and went far. The traveler had high hopes of a speedy journey. But the second morning these jungle tribesmen refused to move. For some strange reason they just sat and rested. On inquiry as to the reason for this strange behavior, the traveler was informed that they

had gone too fast the first day, and that they were now
waiting for their souls to catch up with their bodies.[4]

How would you know if your body has outrun your soul? We have talked about not being able to feel, but how about not being able to pray or cry or do nothing but cry? Maybe you don't have any interest in spiritual things. Or you don't laugh anymore or sing along to your favorite song. Church is boring. People are annoying. Nothing sounds fun. You just want a vacation, but come to think of it, most of those have all been pretty miserable. Getting dressed up is a chore. You hate the holidays. You've gained twenty pounds.

Or maybe it's none of the above except this sinking feeling that when all the running stops, you've got nothing. Empty. *Nada.* Nothing to give and nothing to dream and mostly nothing to become. If life seems to have left you empty, I'd say you can be sure that your body has outrun your soul.

Jesus came so that we can have life in all its fullness—remember John 10:10? You have been given fullness in Christ (Colossians 2:10). He promises to fill everything in every way (Ephesians 1:23). That you will be filled with the fruit of righteousness (Philippians 1:11). So that you might be filled to the measure of all fullness by the love of God (Ephesians 3:19).

Jesus modeled for us a life of spiritual fullness and the necessity to be refilled. Gordon MacDonald wrote:

> *Study the life of Christ, and you will discover that*
> *He was never on the verge of passionlessness. He obvi-*
> *ously understood how one gets into that kind of situ-*
> *ation. It is no accident that before and after heavy*

periods of activity He went apart and stored up, or replenished, the inner energy or passion necessary to carry out His mission. And, again, it is no accident that He never seems to have engaged in activity that was beyond His reasonable limits.[5]

In pursuit of Christ's filling and stopping to be refilled, I am going to ask you to stop for a while. I realize that you are possibly rolling your eyes at me, wondering who appointed me official world stopper. No one, actually. I'm just telling you how God walked me out of fifteen years of numb and back into my life. Stopping your body so that your soul might catch up could very well be one of the most exhilarating things you've ever done. So here you go:

- Continue in the mandatory commitments necessary to care for your family and your career.
- Complete any other time and energy obligations you have made.
- Do not take on any new responsibilities for a determined length of time. I really want you to seek God on the length of time. I feel that it should be extended and sufficient for restoration. Pray it through. Wait until you have heard God.
- Let the people in your life know that you are not accepting new obligations during this focused time of soul care. After a while I didn't even have to explain anymore; I just said, "Thanks so much for thinking of me, but I have made a commitment to take two years off." People looked at me weird, but

I learned to stand my ground, and finally for something that really mattered.

Note to single women: I also decided that during this time I should not pursue an exclusive dating relationship. That was a personal decision based on the healing that needed to begin in my heart. I was afraid that I would make a relationship decision out of my emptiness. I'm sure you now believe I am a total geek, but not dating may not apply to you so pray about it. Turned out to be the easiest New Year's resolution I ever made and kept two years running.

Have you ever heard that stress is when your gut says, *No*, but your mouth says, *Why sure, I'd be glad to?* We're getting ready to cut out some of the stress. Believe me, there will be plenty of time to be room mom and first-base coach and city council advocate later. Actually, you may even enjoy all of those things even more after you have stepped back to locate your heart. I expect you to come out of this season full of the presence of God, aware of His calling on your life, and desperate to know Him more.

> *Though I am always in haste, I am never in a hurry because I never undertake more work than I can go through with calmness of spirit.*
> —John Wesley

Somewhere we've learned that it's wrong for us to focus on our-selves. It *is* wrong to become self-absorbed, egotistical, and narcis-sistic. But in order to dance, the un-woman has to stop and survey where she is and who she's become. Knowing yourself and being honest about who you've become are prerequisites for growth. When you begin to focus on yourself, then you begin to do the work of choosing health and healing. We want to know God's divine strategy for our lives. The details will be different for each ' one of us, but the characteristics of His life in a woman are remark-ably similar.

The woman living inside God's divine strategy is made strong by her complete dependence on Him. She has an abiding, overar-ching sense that she is being guided step-by-step through every decision and circumstance that life presents. She can face even bit-ter disappointment with confidence that she is still completely inside the protection of God's divine will for her life. That's the life I want for you. To want to dance that kind of dance with God. To focus on your heart and your environment and the care of your soul is essential to your becoming.

Now, here's the other side of that instruction. God gives you per-mission to get your life back. And you have permission to do what-ever is necessary to restore the health of your soul. But stopping your body until your soul catches up is not a license to hurt the people you love. This is not about being distant in your counte-nance or drawing difficult boundaries that keep others out. In this season, it's the distracting activity that has to go away for a while.

You will actually need other people more than ever.

Meeting Together

We'll talk more about this later, but this season of next-step discipleship and soul-becoming is not a season of pulling in. We've done
enough of that already. We've wound ourselves tightly into a ball and
rocked ourselves to sleep in the dark. Scripture says that we should not
neglect meeting together (Hebrews 10:25). Please hear me asking you
to stop spinning. Do not hear me asking you to begin turning away
from love or companionship or the body of Christ. Meeting together
and being together is one of the most powerful tools God will use to
refill your heart and bring your soul back to life.

I do not know of one person who has ever been healed crying
alone on her bed in the dark. Every person I know who finds healing for his or her wounds or strength to battle addictions or sin,
finds it in the light of fellowship and love. I know what it feels like
to be nothing and want nothing and care about nothing. You just
want to hide with your heartache and mourn everything you've
lost. Some of that is so appropriate. It is right to grieve for a while
or even a long time, but you cannot stay there and live. There is no
healing in the loneliness. The repetitious silent suffering only feeds
the emptiness until it eventually begins to consume you.

The author of *The Life Model*, James Friesen, wrote:

> *Becoming mature requires bonds between people—*
> *they are the foundation upon which maturity is built.*
> *Bonds are the connections that energize us, motivate*
> *our actions and establish our identities. The receiving-*
> *and-giving exchange in our bonds shapes our view of*
> *what really is important.*

Friesen goes on to say:

> *Love bonds . . . motivate us to remain faithful*
> *under pressure, to help others to be all they were cre-*
> *ated to be, to be willing to endure pain in order to be*
> *close to those we love, and to tell the truth even when*
> *it hurts.*[6]

It is very important for you to continue in relationship and interacting. As simply as I can say it, the first place you need to be in relationship is in your church. God inhabits the praise of His people, and you need to get in on that. This is all I know: God has promised that He will always use His church as an instrument of blessing, healing, and a place where He will abide. Some of you have been wounded by the church or someone in it.

I am reminded of the story Philip Yancey told to begin his book *What's So Amazing About Grace?* Yancey's friend related the account of a woman whose idea of church was anything but safe:

> *A prostitute came to me in wretched straits, home-*
> *less, sick, and unable to buy food for her two-year-old*
> *daughter. Through sobs and tears, she told me she had*
> *been renting out her daughter—two years old!—to*
> *men interested in sex . . . I could hardly bear hearing*
> *her sordid story. For one thing, it made me legally*
> *liable—I am required to report cases of child abuse. I*
> *had no idea what to say to this woman.*

> *At last I asked if she had ever thought of going to a*
> *church for help. I will never forget the look of pure,*
> *naïve shock that crossed her face. "Church," she cried,*
> *"why would I ever go there? I was already feeling ter-*
> *rible about myself. They'd just make me feel worse."* [7]

Hers is an extreme kind of story. But many have similar thoughts toward the church. Your church should not be a danger-ous place to confess your sin and find help for your brokenness. Church is a safe place to encounter God. If you do not attend a safe place, then don't go back to that kind of body. But you've got to make the effort to find your way into a healthy, fairly functional fellowship of believers.

I realize this may not go over so well with the pastor, but for a while, you don't need to volunteer for anything else. If you don't take this prompting to slow down seriously, I can promise that you will remain the un-woman with the un-life. Stop spending your Sunday mornings running around the building like a wild woman, and just sit in the services for a while.

Go to a church where the pastor opens the Bible and teaches you from the Scriptures. You can get topical monologues on the after-noon talk shows. But at church, you need to hear from God, so find one where the leadership is pursuing His heart and depending on His Word for direction. Ask yourself if the leadership is respected for its integrity and spiritual desire, or has it been known for swirling controversy? Does it seem the activities in the church bulletin are for the purpose of personal, spiritual growth and ministry to others, or do they feel like empty programs?

Take your Bible with you to church, and also something you

can write in, like a journal. Expect to hear from your Father. Listen to the sermon He has intended for you every week. Take notes and review them in your time with God at home. Sing the songs. Go down front and let people pray for you. I know I'm pushing it with the "go down front" thing, but healing is on the line here. Remember, we're talking about a healthy church where people really try to live grace and mercy. And beyond that, we're trying to get your life back.

I remember the first time I stepped out into the aisle and made my way trembling to the front of our church. I was crying so hard I couldn't see. Someone took hold of my arm and began to pray. When I finally looked up, about thirty people had gathered around me, holding me and praying in turn. Do you know what it feels like to be prayed for? Would you just give the body of Christ a chance? Let some people step underneath your burden with you (Galatians 6:2). Let some people pray what you cannot even begin to speak for yourself (James 5:16).

The presence of God is promised when His people have gathered together (Matthew 18:20). And you want to get yourself into God's presence every time you have the opportunity.

I travel almost every weekend to speak to women, but it has become very important for me to be in my church on Sunday morning. Sometimes it's just not possible, but every time I can, I'll take crazy flights that get in at all hours of the night just so I can be with my people. God truly ministers to me there. I realize that meeting together with the people of God may have been difficult for you in the past. Maybe you have suffered wounds from the not-so-well-intending. But do not neglect this instruction to meet with the people of God and hear consistently from the Word of God.

I'm sure you realize that we're just getting started. It will take a while for the wallflower to begin to unfold. Learning to dance will be worth all the effort, I promise.

As we begin, I've asked you to stop much of the distracting activity so that your soul can catch up, and to maintain relationship and fellowship with a healthy, Bible-teaching church. We will talk more about church and the importance of these believers in your life later.

Before each chapter, stop and pray about what you have been reading. Journal your thoughts. Your weakness. Your hesitation. These steps are all bound into one book, but they will probably take months to work down into your soul.

Don't be afraid to go slow if you need to. Wait for God. Feel His tenderness toward you.

My friend Dennis called me on the phone that day and said, "I'm going to tell you exactly what to do." I drank in every word so deeply because I just needed someone to step into my darkness, take me by the hand, and guide me out. I trusted Dennis in those days as my spiritual mentor, and he has continued with me for the past years, walking alongside me through the spiritual renewal God is bringing.

It would be my privilege to mentor you from my lessons, talking you out of the un-life and back into your God-life. Maybe you have already heard the voice of the Father in these beginning words. Maybe your soul has begun to sense a flicker of hope. *There is a way out. There is more.* I am praying that you will hear God calling you back. In the next chapters, I'll keep holding your hand, and we'll keep taking steps out of the shadows and toward His voice together.

a dancing lesson

When we are first learning to dance,
it's always better to have someone
to take you by the hand and
whisper softly in your ear, "No
worries; just watch me, follow
my lead. I am going to teach you
exactly what to do."

WHAT IF THE WOMAN I have always dreamed of becoming is the woman God envisioned when He dreamed of me?

I TRIED TO BE STRONG because I thought it was required, but I have finally heard God say, "You have My permission to need love, to need healing, to need laughter, to need Me."

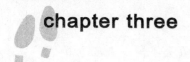

chapter three

Coming Out of the Dark

There is a way God works that has been observed through the ages. People have handed down this truth from generation to generation. It's an adage that we use to comfort one another. In difficult times, we say that *healing takes time.*

I realize that I don't know your wounds or the circumstances that caused them. I don't know the particulars of your private struggles or the pain that pushed you into the dark. But I do know this: Our God heals. Our God restores. Our God redeems. Our God makes all things new. He asks us to choose His healing and then surrender to His process. But we cannot rush through ten steps and expect to be healed. We cannot microwave what generations have watched God do over time.

Getting your life back and beginning to dance will probably require more time than you had hoped. You can't read quickly through this book or any book and lay it down all healed. There is no high-speed Internet access to all the answers. There is no supplement at the health-food store for soul filling. This kind of discipleship and growth requires a concerted effort over time. As we keep taking these little steps, just take a deep breath and settle in. Ask God to give you surrender. Maybe you can pray something like this:

> *God, I want to be able to choose You, to choose heal-*
> *ing and then make it so. I want my life back and my*
> *heart made new so badly. I realize that I could rush to*
> *heal and rush to become and miss the soul filling You*
> *want to bring. This day I will surrender to the process of*
> *time. I will lay down my hurried expectations. I'm*
> *choosing to wait for You and wait for the healing You*
> *will bring as time goes by. Amen.*

There is a woman who got divorced less than a year ago. She loves God, and so the whole thing was incredibly embarrassing. As a Christian, she never expected this to happen to her. She was sure they'd be able to work through anything that came along.

But now, ten months after the divorce was final, she believes the wounds of losing a twenty-two-year marriage have all been healed, and she is planning her marriage to a man twenty years younger. All her friends want her healing to be the real deal, but they can see that in her rush to push through the pain, she is instead choosing to reestablish her value, prove that she is beautiful, and make the old guy who dumped her wish he hadn't. It seems she is skipping over the deeper work that needs to happen in her heart.

A mom lost her teenage son to leukemia. The illness consumed four very long years in the life of their family. It's been a year and a half since his death, and she wonders when she'll want to do anything again. The desire to dance died with her son, and one day at a time is still almost more than she can do. This kind of loss requires a deep healing work in the soul. That kind of healing comes only as time goes by. We cannot rush God's hand.

A lifetime of bad habits and poor choosing brings complicated consequences that take an awful lot of time to unwind.

I wish I could offer you instant everything. Instant healing. Instant maturity. Instant courage. But we did not become un-women in a second. It will take time to untangle the heart. As healing time goes by, I want to give you some of the intentional steps we can take together.

Becoming Intentional

A good friend of mine named Grant died tragically a couple of years ago. After the funeral I was sitting with another friend, Jim. We were recounting the huge impact Grant's life had made on both of us. Jim said, "Ang, look at my cell phone. Last week, Grant and I had lunch. That day I changed the greeting on my phone to remind me of the conversation we'd just had." Jim's cell phone said: *Be Intentional.* Everyone who knew Grant would tell you he lived an intentional, passionate life. He made all of us want a great, big life like the one he lived.

I forget to live intentionally. I don't mean to; I just do sometimes. The kids are home from school today and they get me confused. William was standing beside my bed before the sun was up making a list of all the things he wanted to do. The boys have decided on the dollar movie. Taylor wants to go to Kayla's house, and AnnaGrace wants to have lunch at the tearoom. I have fifty e-mails to return, a book to write—in case no one noticed—and in the middle of all this, somebody has to feed people.

Nobody in my house really cares if I love God or care for my soul today. They love me, but my healing and maturing are not on their list. I was going to live intentionally today, and it could feel like all the people are getting in my way. But that's the point. Your life is just as outrageous as mine. No one will choose intentionally for you or me. We have to wake up and keep choosing for ourselves.

I think the heart of Jim's greeting is that we *keep* pursuing an intentional life. I don't want to get blown around by the kids today and miss a purposeful day. A part of it will involve caring for them and negotiating our schedules, but a part of today's intentional living must involve caring for my soul and my body. Even in the spin of our lives, I am giving priority to healing and spiritual maturity.

I am going to keep putting myself in the presence of God by prayer. It may be chaos on the outside, but the chaos is not making a home inside me ever again. I am not going to let my priorities stay out of order. Something may shove them around from time to time, but I am going to keep setting them straight. I am going to be intentional about the care of my soul.

I realize that you can mean to be intentional and then forget. So let's commit to whatever it takes to remember. We are going to be intentional about healing. We will intentionally choose spiritual maturity. We are going to learn how to dance.

But the years are going by. So change the greeting on your cell phone. Tape a note to your mirror. Paint the words over the kitchen sink. Keep reminding yourself that dancing with God is a deliberate choice of your heart.

Connecting the Dots

I wish I could tell you that the past few years have just flown by and that I've been intentional, growing by leaps and bounds every single day. Actually, it would be very cool if I were almost a spiritual giant by now. Unfortunately, the way out of being an un-woman is many days just hanging on to God as the hours go past. Just connecting the dots. Doing what is in front of you until you can figure out the next right thing.

There are still days when I have to connect the dots until I can find my way. Take the kids to school. Put in a load of laundry. Pay a few bills. Make my bed. Wipe the kitchen counter again. Dot to dot until I can see the bigger picture and find my place. Sometimes we have to resort to doing something simple until we can get the bigger picture going.

Don't be afraid of days that start with you just connecting the dots. Sometimes after a very emotional encounter or an exhausting conversation about your place in life, all you can do for a while are the little things that require minimal thought or feeling.

While we're on the subject, now would be a good time to dial back your expectations for a while. You do not have to keep up with any of the other empty un-women in your life. I am going to be a gourmet cook again, but not now. I'm going to travel for fun, but not yet. Just let some of it go for a season. I tried to keep a lot of extra interests spinning from my emptiness, and it almost sent me under.

You can try to keep it all spinning, too, but eventually they will lock us up in a white room and someone will come in the afternoons to feed us pudding from a plastic spoon. Until you get to the next place, the place we're going together called "healthy woman with a full dancing soul," it's exactly right to lay down most of your huge self-imposed expectations.

Most days my kids go to school in wrinkled shirts. I spend almost every day I'm home in no makeup and gym shorts and with ponytail hair. I pick up soup from the market and put it with a salad from a bag. I don't get to write handwritten thank-yous as often as I'd like to or spend time shopping for just the right gift. Sometimes an e-mail thank-you or an online order is the best I can do for now. In many ways, I've had to lay down a lot of good intentions and just connect the dots for a while.

I love ironed clothes and beautiful dinners and having my hair styled. But I cannot do it all every day and care for my soul. I am deciding my soul and the souls of my children matter more. My being peaceful when I'm with them matters more than anything else. Sometimes it's more peaceful to drive through for chicken-Caesar wraps than to kill myself for homemade. I desire that part of my life, but I am also in a ridiculously busy season of mothering. Right now it just feels so good to have my heart back. I don't want to run ahead of myself and sacrifice any of the growth I've fought so hard to achieve.

Some days it's an accomplishment to connect a few dots. I want you to have permission just to connect the dots for a while and be intentional every time you can. They should give away medals for that.

Someone to Talk To

The best reminders I have of my decision to choose an abundant, full life in Christ are my friends. I have some very cool friends who are at least ten giant steps ahead of me with God. They live wrapped up in the banner of His love. They consistently, tenderly, and firmly stand for God in all circumstances and through all manner of trials. Because they live intentionally, I am reminded.

I watch my friends intentionally parent in strength, and then I am reminded to parent the same. When my girlfriend intentionally takes on a new adventure, then I am motivated to find courage for my adventures. And when a friend talks to me about a new truth from God, good grief, I want to get in on that too!

It's virtually impossible to grow up without someone to talk to. You may stop your life and begin to weed out the distractions. You may be at a great church. Intentional some days and connecting dots others. But I believe strongly that you are going to need someone beside you for these lessons.

I have three friends who almost daily interact with me about my heart, the work God is doing, and my pursuit of spiritual truth. I've mentioned Dennis, who lives on the other side of the country. My two girlfriends also live far away. We spend time together a few times a year, so most of our friendship happens by phone. I have a counselor here in town, my pastor, and lots of great friends, but these mentoring, discipling friends just don't live close.

As you begin to think about who could walk alongside you for this season, I want you to consider the following:

- It is helpful to have a relationship with someone who is at least ten years older. The wisdom that comes from ten more years of living will be so valuable to you. Just as we can foresee some of the traps our children could fall into, someone ahead of you will be able to guide you around emotional and spiritual land mines that still wait for you in the dark.
- Make sure your friend's life screams integrity, grace, mercy, forgiveness, and redemption. You do not need

just a rule-keeper or a guilt-giver. We'll talk more
about this later, but a man or a woman of grace has
come to that truth because it has been given in his or
her brokenness. I would probably be afraid of the
perfect person with the perfect life who's never been
through anything messy.

- There are times in your life when the person you open
  your heart to should only be another woman. If your
  marriage is difficult, the strong advocate for your
  heart should only be a woman. If you are struggling
  with sexual temptation or healing from sexual abuse,
  again wisdom dictates that your discipling friend be
  a woman.

- A person who loves you is the best place to begin.
  Your Father in heaven is wildly in love with you, and
  the love of another person transfers so much of the
  Father's heart.

- Has this person sustained your respect over time?
  Do they model a consistent, growing pursuit of God?
  You need someone who can provide consistent
  strength and vision. Do you remember the old adage
  Whoever you spend time with is who you become? There
  is so much truth packed into those words. The strong
  spiritual people in your life must be farther along than
  you and passionate in their pursuit of God. You are
  not the teacher here. You want to learn from their
  example.

- As a word of caution, a family member could be great
  here, or not. Sometimes we need the kind of

perspective that someone outside our immediate family can give. They've seen you wounded. They've waded through your mistakes. Sometimes they might want you to act too fast or never at all. Sometimes they cannot forgive where you need to. Love your family. Choose your mentors with discernment.

- This is the person who has permission to speak into your soul. Take it seriously, and intentionally decide who will be granted entrance into your heart.

I want to tell you more about Dennis, so you'll have a better picture of the kind of person I'm talking about. Dennis is going to love that I'm telling you he's in his early fifties. About ten years ahead of me. He pastors a church in Southern California where he and his wife serve with the purest hearts for ministry I have ever known. This guy has a great, big love for people, and he desperately wants them to have a healthy, growing relationship with God. He is not afraid of broken lives or messy people or the wild stories they bring into his office. He's a lot like Jesus that way.

I have watched him consistently pursue God for the past twenty years. I have watched him walk through trials and heartache with great integrity. I have heard about the disappointments he has faced and yet, his heart toward God remains tender. He could accumulate stuff, but instead, he and Karen give their stuff away and their time away and their hearts away over and over. He could work harder at remaining comfortable, but I keep watching him jump into the trenches no one wants to be in.

There were days in my darkest hours when I talked to Dennis every few hours. He said, "If you need another breath, just call me.

We'll talk until you can breathe." We started at learning to breathe again, and now he thinks it's the coolest thing that I'm really dancing.

We speak at least once a week now. I talked to him yesterday. I run career decisions past him. He doesn't know anything about publishing, but he knows a lot about the heart. He keeps me true to my heart. I get ministry advice and parenting advice. But mostly, Dennis points me to Jesus. Consistent. Unswerving. Faithful. Come to Jesus; come to Jesus.

I want you to have someone who will consistently say the name of Jesus to you and for you and over you. I want you to be able to lean into the strength of another. Remember, healing doesn't happen in the dark. Your healing and maturing will happen inside the context of strong relationship. When a strong woman of God steps into your life, she brings the light of Christ with her.

Maybe you don't think you have a Dennis anywhere in your life. Maybe not yet. You have been made for friendship and companionship. You and I grow because of those relationships. God knows all of that, and I believe with all my heart that He will provide for you. You must pray and begin to consciously seek that person. I realize you can go forward without them, but these friends have been so integral in my discipleship that I want you to receive the same kind of mentoring and guidance I have known.

Restoring Order

I can't think when things are messy. Really, I have this whole little ritual thing I go through before I can actually sit down and write. I read the paper and fold a load of clothes. Organize the stacks on my desk. Read my Bible. Write in my journal. Go upstairs and brush my teeth again. Look at my calendar. Work on my to-do list. It's a version of piddling and connecting the dots that actually gets me over into thinking and making the words happen. It feels as if I have to get my arms around my life every morning and then I can take the next few steps.

In much the same way, I believe we have to get our arms around the bigger picture of our lives before we can take the next steps of growth. As we are beginning, I believe the essential first work will involve restoring order to your daily life. If you turn around and look at the closets of your soul, I imagine you're afraid to look at the doors bulging with clutter and disarray. You don't even want to know what's in there, much less take the time to make any sense of it all.

I talked to a woman a few months ago who had gotten herself into some of the biggest life messes you can imagine. She was literally losing everything, all at the same time. She couldn't think or even begin to start untangling the wreckage she had caused. She said, "Angela, my whole life is a mess. I don't even have any clean clothes and I haven't paid the bills and the sink is full of dirty dishes." As you already know, all that overwhelming, outward disorder is a direct reflection into the soul.

I asked her, "What can you go home and do right now?"

She said, "I could do the laundry."

"Start there," I offered. "Begin to restore some physical order so that you can think."

In the last chapter, I asked you to stop doing anything beyond the necessary so that you could spend an extended amount of time on this soul work. With the time you have begun to reclaim, I want you to start restoring order to your home and your personal life.

You may need to start small and just do what you can, as you can. That's where I was for months. I remember when cleaning out my purse was an accomplishment. But you may be able to jump right into this directive. If your outside world has grown to reflect your inside chaos, I am asking you to begin to revive the place where you live. Reorder your belongings. Brighten up your surroundings. Let the light in.

So, what can you do first?

- Sort out the garage or your closet.
- Give away some clutter or just have the junk hauled off.
- Balance your checkbook and recommit to a financial budget.
- Mow the lawn or weed the flower bed.
- Find the top of your washer and dryer, then put all that stuff where it goes.
- Clean out your car.

You might be thinking to yourself, *I thought we were talking about spiritual maturity?* We are. But if the foundational structure of your life is in chaos and disrepair, then we have nowhere to build.

I had a friend who felt prompted to go through her house and remove any object that might be a reflection of the old, un-woman life she had been living. She threw out music and DVDs and collections she had bought to fill her emptiness. At the same time, she decided to decorate her home with images that reminded her of the light of Christ, her new life with Him, and the hope He promised for her future. She has a lot of stars and cute lamps and beautiful crosses. I love that in restoring order, she began to surround herself with physical reminders of the One who was leading her out.

Maybe restoring order would mean giving yourself more time to think. Maybe you need to turn down the constant, repetitive noise in your life. Turn off the TV. Take at least one day a week without your cell phone. Don't check your e-mail all weekend.

You pray, and I'm sure God will direct. Where does your physical life need stability and rearranging?

Restoring Your Body

I know you didn't want me to bring it up, but I have to. Depressed un-women living un-lives come in all shapes and sizes, but most of us are quite unhealthy. The body and our emotions are so intricately intertwined that I cannot speak to your soul without directing you to give attention to your body. Emotional health feeds physical health, physical health feeds emotional health, and then our spiritual health reflects the mind, body, and soul working together. A part of becoming the women we were meant to be will depend on whether or not we decide to care for our bodies as they were meant to be cared for.

Probably ten years went by and almost every day I whined, *If I could just sleep in, or get a nap or a longer nap, then I'd feel better and have more energy.* One afternoon after a fairly long nap, I lay there groggy without any real sense of new energy and took a nap inventory. Turns out that I'd actually gotten plenty of naps through the years, but in truth, they never really made me feel much better. After spending such a long time in search of the next miracle nap, the obvious finally became clear: another nap wasn't the answer. Dang it all, I really wanted a nap to be enough, but I had plenty of personal research to prove otherwise.

The only thing that has begun to give me renewed energy is to make a concerted effort to care for my physical body. I know—nobody really wants to hear this. Talk to me about comfort food. Let me crawl under my covers and sleep the pain away. Just leave my body out of a book on spiritual growth. But I can't. This wallflower took another step away from un-woman when I realized that I needed a healthy body to go forward.

Here's the problem. The un-woman is tired. And underneath the tired, she's sad and disappointed and without hope. She is unmotivated, and life has grown meaningless. Becoming physically healthy makes a lot of sense. She wants to. She lobs out a few weak tries. But it's just all too much, and besides, why does it really matter?

I'll tell you why it matters. It matters because deep inside your heart you do not want to live like this. You want to feel strong. You want to have energy and renewed vision for your own life and for the ones you love. You want to see a muscle again. As we begin this journey toward God, I believe it is imperative to begin removing every obstacle to full health in your life. Your physical body really matters.

On my first day back in a gym in who knows how long, I met my new trainer, Clayton. Right off the bat I explained to Clayton that I was officially the biggest pansy he'd probably ever met. It was my insecure way of lowering any unrealistic expectations he might have.

He seemed undaunted by the pansy challenge and led me to the weigh-in, fat-test room.

In the couple of years before I went to see Clayton, I had lost a good amount of weight, but still didn't feel strong or energetic. In the testing room, I found out why. Seems that I was in the size clothing I wanted to wear, it's just that my body fat was a whopping 29 percent. Guess that diet of Sprite and Raisinettes hadn't been as good as I thought.

Thankfully, Clayton didn't act as though I was the worst thing he'd ever seen, but my body fat explained everything about why I was sluggish and my fatigue seemed overwhelming.

That day he handed me a strict diet that alternates every other day. A list of vitamins he recommends for women and then the physical exercise he felt I needed to begin and maintain to see if we could find a muscle underneath the flubber. Body fat had to go down; muscle mass had to increase. I began weight training three days a week and getting some cardio on the days in between. I had already checked with my doctor, and she was more than happy to give me the green light.

I have to tell you, beginning to care for my physical body is truly making me feel stronger, unlike the decade-long nap pursuit. Sometimes as women, we have relegated our physical care to the very last place of priority. I completely understand. There is no time. No money. No encouragement. People look at you funny. It's just that most of those people want the same thing you do, but can't figure out how to get started or keep going.

Here's my advice for getting started. Go anyway. We could spend a two-hour lunch exchanging all the reasons we do not have time or the inclination. Go anyway. The kids might smirk. Go anyway. Your husband might look at you like you're cross-eyed. Go anyway. Your workout clothes might feel too tight. Go anyway. You might not have any hope that this time you'll stick to it. Go anyway.

Choose the thing that seems most interesting to you. Club, trainer, national fitness plan, Pilates, or dance classes. And then just go. I never had any luck sticking to exercise at home by myself. Making an appointment with someone who knows my name and expects me to show up is strong accountability for me. If I get on his calendar for three days next week, I'm going to get there because I promised that I would. I have the same accountability when I promise my neighbor we'll walk together. She expects me. I don't feel like going, but I show up anyway because she's my friend.

As a woman who is working on restoring her body, I am learning to take hormones into consideration. The older I get, the more I'm affected by the cycle of fatigue and strength. At this age, I can finally anticipate that every four weeks I'm going to be plowed over by the PMS freight train. I absolutely hate it, and every single month I think, *It's not going to get me this time.* But PMS always knocks me flat. Finally, I'm learning just to go with it. Take ibuprofen for three days, exercise anyway, and keep my schedule light.

Would you spend some time praying about how to care for your body? The soul healing we desire is going to take time. But a good beginning requires you to stop and seek God for the restoration that's essential to becoming a strong, confident woman.

You Believe What You Focus On

As I'm writing to you, I realize that instead of beginning to take these necessary steps toward growth, you are probably like me and tempted to keep playing the same old lines in your head: *Not now. Maybe later. You don't get my life. I'm overwhelmed. It's too much. I've already failed so many times.* Those very kinds of thoughts have already stolen too much of my own life, and I refuse to live the next forty years in the prison they can build around my heart.

What I've learned is that you begin to believe what you focus on, whether it's actually true or not. I have personally focused on my rejection in various areas of career and relationships and then began to live as though I was worthy of only rejection. I have believed what I have focused on. That trash is a complete mind game formulated by Satan to steal our dreams and our confidence. That kind of mental garbage will take you down and keep you there. But it's all a lie.

These mistaken beliefs will limit and frustrate the work God intends to do. What focus have you allowed to become a negative, limiting belief? What kind of mind game is Satan playing with you? You will never be loved? Never be godly? Never have order in your private world? Never have confidence?

I want your focus to change. Actually, nothing will happen, I mean a big, fat *nothing*—until you begin to focus on the truth of God. The wallflower stands along the edge of her life believing the lies she's heard in her head all her life. She focuses on every flaw and limitation. She sees only why she can't. God says, *I'm so in love with you. I made you for dancing. You can do anything inside the strength of My love. You are worthy. You are capable. You are beautiful.* Until you decide to change your focus, your beliefs will never change.

You cannot keep telling yourself some big story. In two years, you'll still be talking about the same old things. This is the day. You have to change your focus and just begin to come to Jesus. Oswald Chambers wrote:

> *If you want to know how real you are, test yourself*
> *by these words—"Come unto Me." In every degree in*
> *which you are not real, you will dispute rather than*
> *come, you will quibble rather than come, you will go*
> *through sorrow rather than come, you will do anything*
> *rather than come the last lap of unutterable foolish-*
> *ness—"Just as I am."* [1]

Do away with the distractions. Get a spiritual adviser, friend, teacher. Take very literal steps to bring order to your physical world and your physical body so that you can begin to center your life on Jesus. I believe you can do this, because I know the power of God to make it so. Decide with me to believe God more than anything.

Wallflowers who make God their focus get to dance.

❧

Maybe it seems we should just be able to skip past some of these thoughts and get on to the soul, but we can't. Look around you. Do you have a friend you can talk to? Does your home need to be restored? Does your body need to be renewed? Have you only believed what you've focused on? We cannot ignore your environment or your vessel. To push ahead would be unwise. To neglect their care would mean building on a faulty foundation.

In applying these lessons, you are taking very literal and life-transforming steps in the direction of healing. The wallflower is stepping out of the shadows. Time will go by. I can't wait for you to see what God does as you continue to take steps of physical and spiritual growth.

a dancing lesson

The wallflower has to decide to reach down
and unfasten the cords that have kept her tied
to the chair. One strap at a time. Orderly.
Over time.

Until she's

free.

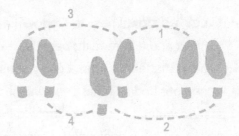

HOW MUCH MORE is done by the blood of Christ. He offered himself through the eternal Spirit as a perfect sacrifice to God. His blood will make our consciences pure from useless acts so we may serve the living God.

—Hebrews 9:14 NCV

LET US COME near to God with a sincere heart and a sure faith, because we have been made free from a guilty conscience, and our bodies have been washed with pure water. Let us hold firmly to the hope that we have confessed, because we can trust God to do what he promised.

—Hebrews 10:22–23 NCV

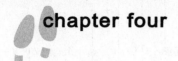

chapter four

A Clean Life

lmost everywhere I go and in lots of the interviews I do, people ask me the same question: "How do you do everything? How do you take care of the children, write, and speak?" I used to say, "I fly by the seat of my pants. Somehow it all comes together and God takes care of us."

Ever since I had children, the "seat of my pants" thing has been true. I just barely get everything done and consciously choose to leave many things undone. But in the past few years there has really been something else going on; there is a deeper God-relationship that is making my life different. I want to find the words to try to explain to you the soul peace I have been given right in the middle of our chaos. I wear all the same hats that you do, and honestly, there is rarely ever a day without several hat changes. Being a mom could take from me every ounce of energy and compassion I have to give. Speaking and writing could do the same, only with jet lag.

I have walked with God for at least twenty-five years, but I began to ask myself: *What is making the past few years different and stronger*

*even though I have known more brokenness, pain, and seeming attack
than ever? Why is there a more profound assurance of God's presence,
unlike any other season of my life? How am I making it?*

Several years ago, I did begin to connect the dots, choosing to
take the steps to restore order to my home and my body. A strong
foundation is being rebuilt because of the ongoing restoration, but
I realize that an ordered life is not the whole answer. I could become
a very organized woman with a healthy body, lots of muscles, and
yet empty of the power and presence of God. I believe that I am
beginning to live a full life, operating inside the kingdom abundance Jesus offered because of several spiritual elements that have
been taught to me, cultivated, and finally implemented.

One of those elements is the idea that God wants you and me
to live with a clear conscience. He gives power and strength to a
clean life and a consistent pursuit.

A Clear Conscience

Paul was a follower of Christ. One whom God used powerfully.
His life and God-breathed message have shaped the way every generation of Christians that came after him would learn to live in relationship and obedience to God.

One day I was reading through the book of 2 Timothy. I got
to the end, but kept going back to reread some of the beginning
words. Evidently, Paul thought it was very important for us to
know that he was serving God with a *clear conscience* (2 Timothy
1:3). This is the same Paul who had also told us that he did not
always do the thing he wanted to do, but the very thing he did
not want to do instead (Romans 7:15). Hmm, a clear conscience.

I knew I'd read that in Scripture before. Why hadn't I paid more attention to its significance?

A few verses later, Paul instructed Timothy to "fan into flame" the gifts God had given to him (2 Timothy 1:6 NIV), reminding Timothy that God does not give a spirit of timidity, but a spirit of power, of love, and of self-discipline (2 Timothy 1:7 NIV).

Obviously a clear conscience was such a vital part of serving that Paul both modeled the character trait in his own life and highlighted its value in his writings. I believe he wanted followers of Christ to understand its importance and give determination to its pursuit. I believe he wanted us to know that a clear conscience is necessary and desirable. Its presence in our lives begins to make a way for our gifts to fan into flame, so that we might operate in the spirit of power he spoke of.

Here's what I know from both personal experience and observation: if your conscience is not clear, then you spend a lot of mental and emotional energy trying to cover things up. The murky conscience requires that a great deal of thinking be devoted to inner wrangling and rationalizing. This burdened conscience is a heavy chain that will keep you shackled to a wall of guilt. It never lets you get very far, and you certainly don't get to dance.

God Makes You Clean

You can't do anything or accomplish anything or begin to grow in strength or confidence when your life is shackled to a wall of guilt. Darkness settles over the heaviness in your heart and holds you hostage there in the confusion. Your conscience is an instrument of the Holy Spirit. It's right to feel guilty over sin or poor choices. That good guilt can prompt us to seek forgiveness and restoration.

But if we choose not to immediately respond to the leading of the Holy Spirit, then our consciences can become so encumbered that we find our lives essentially chained to guilt we've tried to ignore. That kind of prolonged guilt begins to defile our thinking and our emotions.

We live in such a dark society that I think we've come to accept our society's darkness as an unavoidable part of our own. It can begin to feel as if we are required to pull this ball and chain of guilt and private struggle around with us. Besides, it seems everybody else does. But it does not have to be so. We belong to God, and He has made a way for us to live in the light. We can live with a clear conscience because of the freedom Christ gives. We can pursue a clean life even if no one else around us wants to go there, and even if others continue to remind us of our mistakes. We do not have to be shackled to guilt and the shame of poor choices for a lifetime. Because of Jesus, we can serve God with a clear conscience.

This has possibly been one of the most difficult next-level truths of God for me to personally receive and apply. All the time God has been yelling to me, "I want to set you free! I want to make you clean. I'm sending a Savior. I am moving heaven and earth to get to you." And for most of my life I have rejected this kind of freedom from guilt.

> *Then I will sprinkle clean water on you, and you*
> *will be clean. I will cleanse you from all your unclean-*
> *ness and your idols.*
>
> (Ezekiel 36:25 NCV)

Guilt seemed righteous somehow. And maybe if I just kept flogging myself before God, He'd be happier with me because of my shame. God was probably always mad at me about something anyway, and it was my job to uncover what God would be mad at me about next. Besides, how in the world could anyone ever have and maintain a clear conscience? Sounds haughty and arrogant, like something only an apostle could say.

Come to find out, most women feel much the same way and struggle with the application of this truth. Not so long ago a woman asked to have breakfast with me. She was single and had allowed herself to act inappropriately with a man she had been dating. Brokenhearted over her mistake, we sat together and sorted things out. She was mad at herself, frustrated by her poor choosing, and aching over her shame before the man and before God. We talked through her obvious repentance, prayed together, and I am sure that she received God's complete forgiveness that morning.

About eight months later she came to me again. Still grieving the same sin of that one night. Still flogging herself.

"Has anything happened since we last talked?" I asked. "Have you made similar choices again? Has that night become a pattern for you in any way?"

"No," she spoke through her tears. "It was just that one time, but I still live with such shame and regret. I'm reminded all the time of my blatant disobedience to God."

"Do you remember the morning that we prayed and asked God for His forgiveness?" I asked.

She nodded her head that she remembered.

"Then tell me what we have if the forgiveness of God does not truly forgive?"

My friend said nothing.

"Look at me," I gently persuaded. "You have been forgiven. Your conscience is clear. The accuser wants you to live in shame and weakness because of your mistake. Eight months have gone by, and you could have been living grateful for the forgiveness God has given. It's time to lift your head up. God has made you clean."

God's Forgiveness

Here's how I have come to feel about the pursuit of a clear conscience. Either the forgiveness that God has promised to us is half-hearted and conditional, based on some unattainable, unknown standard of self-flogging and sustained guilt, or His forgiveness really forgives—instantly, eternally, and completely.

Either I believe that forgiveness is what God said—free, available to any who would call on His name, and completely able to cleanse the impure heart—or I don't really believe God. Either God can make you clean or He is not God.

I am staking my whole life on the belief that God is who He says He is. Jesus is really His Son, my Savior. His death was enough to pay the penalty for every sin. His resurrection was the proof of His divinity. The Holy Spirit is His promised gift to you and me for day-by-day, moment-to-moment guidance. And for some reason that doesn't make any sense to anybody, God is so crazy in love with His creation that He freely forgives any who would ask. In case you haven't thought about it lately, when the God of heaven and earth forgives there is nothing that can happen to make it less, and there is nothing you can do to make it more. Forgiven in the name of Jesus means your conscience is clear.

That truth is why we get down on our hands and knees and worship the only One who is able to cleanse us from all unrighteousness. That's why we show up at church and persuade our friends to come to Bible studies and try to rearrange our lives around God. That's what makes God amazing and takes our breath away at His generosity. That is why we sing and lift our hands to thank Him for the gift of being forgiven. When God bends down in His mercy and forgives a helpless, little, beat-up woman like you or me, then no matter what anyone says or how many voices you hear in your head or how long it takes you to believe it, you have been made clean. You are forgiven.

It's time to hold your head up.

It's time to dance.

The Battle I Tend to Forget

In case you haven't thought about it in a while, I want to remind you that growing up, living a clean life, and becoming a mature woman of God is a spiritual battle. Satan absolutely does not want you to have a clear conscience or a clean life. He does not want your growth to happen. If you are running after God, then I can assure you, there's a big red target on your back. And if you're under thirty, I think the target is triple-sized.

I watch my teenage daughter and her friends. I meet with single women who are in their dating years. Satan is on the loose, and he wants to inflict as many wounds as he can as early as he can. He knows those wounds can hound you for life. He knows the choices you make in these early years can traumatize your marriage and ruin your confidence. The target is bigger because he wants to hurt you as much as possible as soon as he can.

I know this might sound crazy, but for many years a spiritual battle was the last thing I would think of. I would forget that Satan wants my mind and my heart. He wants me to remain in emptiness or walk around feeling numb and overwhelmed. He wants to destroy my passion and kill every dream God has given to me. He wants my children. He wants to sneak into our home. He wants the presence of evil to begin to feel normal to us. He cannot have my soul, but he will settle for my life.

Sometimes I will walk out of a meeting or away from a personal encounter feeling so discouraged. The numbers might indicate that business isn't going well. The next steps in a relationship aren't always clear. The input from others can seem muddled or confusing. It's uncomfortable to be deflated and still have to face conflict or decisions. It always makes me want to give up and run away. But eventually I will begin to hear this list of questions running through my head:

- *Do you love God? Yes.*
- *Do you want to honor Him with your life? Yes.*
- *Are you living clean? Yes.*
- *Is your conscience clear? Yes.*

*Then get back in there and fight for goodness
until you see the glory of God.*

I said to my friend the other day, "If being grown-up is about my comfort, then I'm ready to take my ball and go home. I'm tired and my feelings are hurt and I'd just rather not be bothered with trying to make sense of people and circumstances. But if this is for the glory of God, then let's keep going. I want to be grown-up in Jesus."

We fight the good fight so that the glory of God can be revealed, both in our personal lives and in the public testimony of our faith. I believe that a huge piece of the battle goes to this idea of a clear conscience and a clean life.

Who can have you when you're clean? No one. They can accuse you. They can gossip about you. Plans can fail. But when your heart is good and everything is on the table, out in the light, then God prevails. He can use a woman like that. He will be glorified in her.

I think I forget about the battle because I am not a fighter. I am happy to be a woman, so when it comes to fighting I'm sure that I fight like a girl. Except now that I am a mom, I think I could fight like a heavyweight for my children. I have avoided fighting all of my life. I realize there are some women who like to fight. I've met a few of them. But most of us don't really rise to the occasion. Nothing about the term *spiritual battle* makes me want to lace on the gloves. More often than not, I'd rather just run away until the trouble has passed and let somebody else fight for me.

I'm sure my aversion to fighting has kept me from spiritual

growth. In the past, Satan could say *Boo!* and I'd retreat. But a woman who is growing in maturity realizes there is a battle going on, and there are times when all that can be done is to fight your way through or out.

Satan wants to keep you from a clean life. Some days we'll have to fight the good fight to make it so.

Shackles

If you want a clear conscience, God makes it simple. Ask, receive, and then choose to live clean, being made clean again and again by the ongoing process of repentance and receiving God's forgiveness.

Here's the hard part. For many of us, a clear conscience is going to take some work. There is a lot of cleaning that needs to happen. There is a whole lot more going on than just not receiving God's forgiveness eight months ago or eight years ago. My friend Mark Pate says there are two types of sin:

1. Not obeying, which is the sin of rebellion; and
2. the sin of presumption, or going ahead when God has not issued a directive, which always has consequences.

Whether it's the sin of disobedience or presumption, there are sin patterns to deal with, core beliefs that have to be radically changed, and a lifestyle that must be transformed with the truth of God's call to clean living. Not so many are up for the work. And a lot of the "more hip" Christians I meet think it's unnecessary. Grace allows them freedom to do everything. I am probably getting ready to alienate some folks, but bear with me. A woman told me recently that she is more liberal in her faith than I am. In that particular conversation, what she meant was that she believes she is free to pick and choose her sin. Come on, what is that?

I am, without a doubt, so incredibly imperfect. Ask anybody who knows me or puts up with me or lives with me. But it would be even more ridiculous of me to stand in front of God and begin to rationalize my sin in the name of liberal faith. I am a sinner, but I don't think the sin part is okay with God.

I guess my patience is becoming weary of our ambiguity. Either we are going to grow up and become mature women, or we are going to remain whiney, saved but sloppy, spiritually going around in circles, watching the days of our empty lives go by.

There are things God has asked us not to do because we belong to Him. We carry inside these vessels the living presence of the Holy Spirit. We have been set apart and called to be different. We reflect His heart to a very lost and sick world. At the very least we cannot come to believe it's okay to continue in our sin. We cannot act like the rest of the world.

We have not been called to blend in, looking and sounding just like we did before we knew Christ. Don't you remember? We live in this world, but we are no longer of this world. People should be able to tell the difference. It takes a lot of mental calisthenics and emotional energy to cover an unclean conscience or blatant choices that go against the heart of God.

When you and I allow darkness or choose darkness, we are also choosing to remain spiritually immature. It's virtually impossible to go forward with God when you are spending most of your time covering what keeps you unclean.

Every weekend I talk to women who wish they could go forward personally, or in their marriage, but find that they can't. I will ask some basic questions like:

- Is your heart clean before God?
- Is your conscience clear?
- Have you done what you need to do to make things right?
- Have you done the hard work of forgiveness?

I'm always surprised that women will many times respond, "No." They had just wanted me to say something that let them skip this part, but I couldn't. God calls us to live clean.

Most of the Christian women I know are smart enough not to choose poorly in public. Their shackles are private, and they spend inordinate amounts of time and energy trying to hold back the darkness they play with. As you know, darkness is a powerful element. It begins to take over from the inside out, eventually pushing out most of the light. It is very easy to wake up one sunny day, completely overtaken by the dark.

I'm going to list for you some of the chains I've heard about recently from women who whisper to me through their tears. As you read through these observations, I want you to pay special attention to any prompting the Holy Spirit might give to you.

- Women are having illicit sex, both single and married, young and old, Christian and non. And/or they are spending way more time than we've previously believed fantasizing about having an affair or an inappropriate relationship. We always used to think that was just for men.

- Many Christian women are involved in lesbian relationships, both sexual and emotional. Maybe they have not consummated their relationship with the physical act of sex, but their emotional dependence has become an unhealthy attachment. An attachment that should have been reserved for a husband in a marriage relationship.

- There is a dangerous proliferation of pornography weaving its way into the hearts and minds of women. The images are everywhere and so they almost seem normal to us now. Magazines, films, chat rooms, and the easy access on the Internet to information that no one needs. We would be deceived to believe that pornography is only a man's battle.

- Grown-up women are quietly suffering from eating disorders of all types, trapped inside the cage of "have to be thin at any cost."

- A snare that I have heard a lot about recently involves the private determination to get revenge. In relationships, careers, and families, women have found themselves entangled in a web they have woven by setting traps for others and plotting their private vindication.

- Deeply entrenched anger and all the emotional and physical by-products of its presence privately destroy the hearts of many.

- Reckless spending, gambling, prescription drug use, and alcohol abuse are chains that aren't quite as secret anymore. It's become very common for us to accept these activities in others or in ourselves.

I may not have touched on your particular private battle, but the question for all of us remains the same: *Is your conscience clear?* If you ask yourself honestly and realize the answer is *no*, this next section is for you. If you know that you stand before God with a clean life, you probably already know that a clear conscience is an ongoing, daily commitment to live right and free of guilt before God.

In the past few years, my teenage daughter has chosen to indulge her overabundance of social skills, forsaking the call to higher learning and the grades I know she is able to make. A few weeks ago I got an e-mail from the freshman English teacher at our Christian school: "Taylor is so bright but thought you'd want to know that three weeks into the new semester and she has a 57 average. Is there anything going on that I can pray about for her?" (I'm telling this with Taylor's permission.)

Pray about? I was sure that no praying was necessary. I printed out the e-mail and taped it to her bedroom door. Then I began to map out the consequences.

- Cell phone gone until the end of the semester.
- Instant-messaging her friends was still gone from the last time, but really gone now until Jesus comes back.

- Social outings gone for two weeks, with the possibility of an extension.
- The door to her bedroom on deck to be removed, if grades don't come up by report card time.

I was extremely frustrated with my good kid who did a lot right, but grades continued to be low on her priority list. When I disciplined her, I was stern and she clearly understood the punishment.

And then, nearly a week after her butterfly life had come to an end, I came home one afternoon to find Taylor sitting at my computer talking to her friends on Instant Messenger. She was busted and I wanted to freak out. "Go to your room" was all I could get out. She willfully chose to disregard a very well-known restriction. Evidently she had been sneaking around and, come to find out, this was the "eighth or tenth time" she had used the messenger without permission during this ban.

You can imagine how the mostly one-sided conversation went after I got to her room.

"Does it feel good to deceive?"

"No, ma'am."

"Do you realize that you are choosing to disobey?"

"Yes, ma'am."

"Do you know that you can keep choosing secretly and then one day not even feel bad about it?"

"Yes, ma'am."

"Do you remember how I pray to God?"

"You're praying for us to get caught if we're doing wrong."

"Bingo."

I do pray for my children to get caught. I don't want them to become accustomed to an unclear conscience. And I have begun praying the same for myself.

While I'm not as attracted to blatant disobedience because the pain of getting caught eventually tainted the allure, I could still fall into deception or manipulation. I am just like anyone else, especially when I am tired or overwhelmed, and I could easily fall into excuses or rationalizing my weakness. Daily, I am praying that God will reveal each place of potential sin before it has the opportunity to take hold of me, draw me into darkness, or worse yet, hurt someone else.

God is a loving parent. I see that Taylor could fall into harmful patterns if she is left undisciplined. I'm so very in love with her, and I'd rather make her mad at me than have her walk in foolishness. So I discipline her to protect her. Maybe God has already begun the work of discipline in your life. Maybe you are suffering the consequences of poor choices. If your conscience is not clear, if you find yourself trapped inside a private world that is out of control or out of order, or if you aren't sure that you have ever stood clean before God, here's what I want you to do.

Begin by reading the following verses from the Bible. Listen to God affirm His desire that we live with a clear conscience.

I strive always to keep my conscience clear before God and man.

(Acts 24:16 NIV)

Now this is our boast: Our conscience testifies that we have conducted ourselves in the world, and especially in our relations with you, in the holiness and sincerity that are from God. We have done so not according to worldly wisdom but according to God's grace.

(2 Corinthians 1:12 NIV)

How much more is done by the blood of Christ. He offered himself through the eternal Spirit as a perfect sacrifice to God. His blood will make our consciences pure from useless acts so we may serve the living God.

(Hebrews 9:14 NCV)

Next is the choice to surrender to the process of being made clean. I realize this is probably uncomfortable for you. Nobody wants to have her bedroom door taken off its hinges. But sometimes it's necessary for a season in order to learn how to live when the door is returned.

1. Begin with self-examination. Where are you with God today? What stands in between you and a clear conscience? If you begin to peel back the layers of patterns and habits you've developed over the years, will you find sin that has been hidden or covered?

2. Confess your sin. Private confession for private sins. Public confession for public sins. All sin confessed to God. Private confession happens one-on-one with the one you have offended or hurt. That private confession may need to happen in front of a counselor or in front of a board of elders. But either way, the private confession of private sin remains private. Public confession is required when your disobedience has publicly caused harm to others and to your reputation. The newspaper journalist who has lied in her published reporting would not just confess to her editor. A public confession is required.

There was a time for me when I felt split open from head to toe. I remember begging God to show me anything else. While we were in there looking underneath my pretending, I asked Him to go even deeper and show me anything and everything that kept me from Him. When I am in my private time of confession with God, there is no reason to hold back. I want to be clean, and this process is the only way to get there.

John Ortberg said, "Confession is not just naming what we have done in the past. It involves our intentions about the future as well. It requires a kind of promise."[1]

3. Ask for forgiveness. To confess is one step, but the humbling that comes in asking God's forgiveness is an act of obedience that cleanses. To ask for what we do not deserve also becomes a mile marker of sorts. One that reminds me where I don't want to go again.

4. Receive the mercy. God delights to show mercy. He delights to hold back what you and I have deserved. Receive this gift with gratefulness. God's mercy redeems your life. Listen to the truth of these words and their promise for your life:

> *Redemption is God bringing good out of bad, leading us to wholeness, and the experience of God's amazing power.* Redemption means that out of our greatest pain, can come our most profound personal mission in life.[2]

God can take your confession and do the amazing work of redemption. He can make your life clean and then give purpose to your personal mission. But in order for all that to happen, things really do have to change.

You and I can't stay in the old patterns of deceit and expect to live pure. We can't hang out with the people who led us down the path. We can't visit the same old places anymore. We have to choose light over darkness and have nothing to do with the one who can lure us back with the same old tricks. If it feels like darkness, then it probably is. Choose the light. We remain unclean because we don't want to stay surrendered to examination, confession, and forgiveness. I understand. It's one of the hardest and best things I do.

⌒⌒

I realize this piece of spiritual maturity can be painful and embarrassing. But to continue in an unclean life will bring us to an immediate dead end. There won't be any more growth apart from choosing to live clean. No confidence. No dancing. No grown-up woman with a great, big life. You will never even hear the music.

This day, run into the arms of God. Pray for His tender guidance. Ask Him for a clear conscience and let Him make you clean.

a dancing lesson

With a clean life and a clear conscience,
the wallflower can lift up her head and look
intently into the eyes of the One who has
asked her to dance.

GROWTH IN WISDOM may be exactly measured by decrease in bitterness.

—*Friedrich Nietzsche*

DO NOT BE BITTER or angry or mad.

—*Ephesians 4:31 NCV*

chapter five

Resisting Bitterness, Believing God

Yesterday morning, five minutes before it was time to leave for school, three of my kids looked at the lunch menu taped to the side of the refrigerator and decided they didn't want breaded chicken patties for lunch. I couldn't really blame them. Who in the world would want a breaded chicken patty on a bun? But time was short, and I could offer only peanut butter and jelly sandwiches as a quick replacement. Everybody decided anything was better than a chicken patty, and we began furiously throwing together three sack lunches.

I grabbed the cheese crackers shaped like SpongeBob and filled three snack Ziploc bags, wrapped up some sugar cookies that none of them like, threw in the obligatory piece of fruit that I was sure no one would eat, and passed out quarters to buy milk. We made it. Three packed lunches and still in the car on time.

Grayson, my fifth grader and serious loather of chicken patties, was beside me in the front seat. About the time we got out of our neighborhood, I glanced over at him. He didn't just have that preteen, I'm-grumpy-in-the-morning look on his face. He was mad and on the verge of tears.

"What's going on?" I began gently.

"Mom, this is going to be the worst day ever."

"What do you mean? Did something happen that I don't know about?"

"You gave me the wrong cheese crackers."

"What? There were two boxes, but they're both shaped like SpongeBob. I just used the one that was already open."

"You gave me the Cheese Nips, and the Cheez-Its taste better. Now everything is going to be awful."

Fortunately, I was able to contain the volcanic eruption that instantly began to boil up inside me. We were driving to school and I use this technique sparingly, but as soon as there was an opportunity, I pulled over to a clearing beside the road for special emphasis. Everybody sits up straight and looks really scared when I pull off the road for a spontaneous "Come to Jesus" meeting. They know from previous experience that I could make them get out of the car and walk or any number of other consequences to restore order inside the car.

"Grayson, you need to look at me. Cheese Nips? You're going to have an awful day because of Cheese Nips? Well, let me tell you something. If we have an accident on the way to school, that's an awful day. If somebody you love gets sick and goes to the hospital, that's awful. If a tornado blows our house away, then it's one of the worst days ever. Even chicken patty sandwiches might taste awful, but they cannot cause you to have an awful day. Cheese Nips are crackers. They are nothing. You will have an awful day only because you are choosing to believe that in your mind."

I shot a dramatic glare back to the rest of the children to see if anyone else looked sad enough to get in on this roadside sermon. They all sat there looking very spiritual and grateful for whatever cheese crackers they had.

I'll spare you the rest of the high-pitched talking that involved children around the world who don't have any crackers or a mom to put them into a Ziploc. Needless to say, there was a lava flow of correction pouring out of me that morning, and nobody wanted to be caught in its path.

We got to school and all the kids made a polite mad dash for the door, especially Grayson, but I was on a roll and I couldn't let him go without one more instruction.

"Grayson, I want you to go into that school happy and thankful for every good gift God has given to you. This is not an awful day. This is the day the Lord has made. Believe in Him and His promises to you. I want you to smile at people and walk into your classroom looking for the person who needs your encouragement. I want you to bless people today and give them the light of Jesus."

"Yes, ma'am," he mumbled. I'm sure he kicked himself all the way to homeroom for ever bringing the cracker thing up.

Grayson is eleven. Eleven is difficult for boys. It's a physical and emotional season of transition. Everything is dramatic and difficult. As a family, we're just trying to muddle our way through the best we can. But I can't allow him to fall into patterns that teach him to be quick to anger or depression or hopelessness. I can't let him begin to find comfort in bitterness. He doesn't need to begin playing the victim for attention.

Grayson is just a little kid with a lot more good days than awful ones. I can see that he's immature and childish, but I love him so much that I don't want to leave him that way. It's my job as his parent to pull the car over every time it's necessary to reshape his vision and redirect his heart.

What's a million times more difficult is dealing with the grown-ups who have learned to console their hearts with bitterness.

A Hundred Reasons

Believe me, every person I know could come up with about a hundred reasons to become bitter and remain a perpetually down-trodden victim. They have a lot more than crackers to make them sad. Real-life tragedies have come to them. Awful consequences suffered. More than one person should have to carry. So much disappointment and heartache. And I have my own list of a hundred reasons to become bitter. It could start somewhere with single mom-ness and end with bill-paying, yard-mowing, lonely night frustration.

Hear me in this. I would be the first one in line to give you permission to feel pain over your circumstances, disappointments, or anger. We cannot deny the pain so many of us have known. Life turns out rotten sometimes, and to teach any different would be ridiculous. To act as if we can pretend our heartache away is even worse.

It seems we give up because we can't see God working all things together for good. We fall into whining and complaining because we don't believe His promises are true. We cry, "Woe is me!" because we can't hear His voice anymore. Besides, living as a victim actually gets some people a little sympathy along the way, and bitterness becomes more attractive the more empty you become.

Steve Brown wrote:

> *Bitterness comes from our turning away from the true God . . . Bitterness—characterized by feelings of hatred, envy, resentment, cynicism and severity—begins when one turns from God and it results in a disease that infects others.*[1]

> *Make sure no man, woman, family group, or tribe among you leaves the LORD our God to go and serve the gods of those nations. They would be to you like a plant that grows bitter, poisonous fruit.*
>
> (Deuteronomy 29:18 NCV)

I have decided that some people actually want you to become bitter. They encourage your resentment and feed your self-pity and indignation. They want you to be angry and get revenge. Doom-and-gloom scenarios become the most prominent topics of conversation. They've given in to being bitter, and they want you to be bitter too. Bitterness is not self-contained. It's an infectious disease that harms everyone who comes in contact with it. Then when we're all infected, we can be in the bitter club together and go to dinner and compare bitter notes.

We get some weird satisfaction in revisiting our bitter memories. Reminding ourselves of the ones who have hurt us. Revisiting every time we have been treated unfairly or unjustly. Planning how to get even. Sulking. Brooding. Remembering.

I've certainly been a baby girl all by myself, without any assistance or prodding from anyone. When life catches you off guard, it's so easy to give in to bitterness, to wallow in the failure and brokenness. I too have whined and cried and pouted at life. I have been hurt and rejected. I have been misrepresented and unheard. I'm embarrassed to tell you how easily I've given up some days. I have tasted the root of bitterness, but I have come to regard its comfort as poison.

I do not want to become a bitter old woman. I do not want to remain inward, focused on my grievances. We cannot stay that way and go forward with God. More than anything, I want to be a grown-up woman. I want to become a mature follower of my Lord Jesus Christ.

Here is what I have come to observe about the mature woman in Christ. She feels pain. She suffers great life disappointments. She knows rejection and loss and loneliness. She could give you a hundred reasons why life hasn't turned out or why every day could be awful. But the mature follower is able to resist living in bitterness. I believe she has not surrendered to this desperate attitude because in her grown-up faith she has learned to believe God instead.

There may be a hundred reasons calling each one of us toward bitterness, but I know that believing God—no matter what—is the conviction that will lead us out.

Choosing to Believe

I met a new friend a few years ago. He is a lanky mid-fiftyish guy with a very intense, very secular eighty-hour-a-week career. He is divorced from a mean woman and for ten years he has lived alone, trying to co-parent with someone no one would want to deal with. His children are mad at their mother, and because of it, they've given him plenty of heartache. But the day I met this man, he came through the door happy. I'm not kidding, he was genuinely happy.

This very unassuming, ordinary-to-look-at man stands apart in character and countenance. So happy, in fact, that just his presence lights up every room we've ever been in. Not only that, we're now three years into meetings and programs, and in every encounter we've ever had, his spirit has been consistently and remarkably the same. Peaceful and positive and looking for good. He's fun to be with. All his colleagues hold him in high esteem. He is respected in his profession and regarded as wise and insightful. The man is not bitter, and he's just like you or me; he's got a hundred reasons he could give in to.

One day I took him to lunch to ask the burning questions, "Where in the world did your countenance come from? Are you always happy?"

"Angela, do you think I have a happy-go-lucky, carefree life without any sadness?"

"No, I realize that your life circumstances have been difficult. That's why I'm so interested in hearing about your heart and your thinking. I have rarely met someone like you. Your spirit is full. You radiate a light that touches everyone you meet. Tell me what it is."

"I believe God."

"Somehow, I knew you were going to say that."

Every time I have ever allowed myself to fall into bitterness and disappointment, I realize that I have listened to the prompting of Satan. I have inclined my head toward his directives. I have forgotten that my God is on the throne of all creation. His heart toward me is good. His promises are true. His Son is my Savior. I have forgotten to live what I believe.

Maybe that's where you are today. You realize that you aren't believing God. Maybe you have every earthly right to feel bitter and resentful, but it's been long enough now. It's time to let go of this sickly method of coping. You desire the way out. You want to dance with God toward His plans and His purpose. You want to know a genuine happiness that circumstances cannot stain. If you are tired of bitterness and the despair that it brings, then pay close attention to this next section on choosing. This very day you could be free of bitterness. Not just a little free. You could be finally and fully free.

Choose Freedom

I am tempted to tell you that there are no easy steps to freedom. That there is a process and time involved. There's a learning curve. It'll take a lifetime to get there, but eventually, after a lot of hard work and years of failing, you will choose to believe in the power of God and learn to stay in His freedom.

But I don't really believe that's the way it has to be. I think you can choose to believe God today, and that choosing will radically and powerfully begin to change every aspect of the way you interact with life and the people you love. I have seen the power of God change hearts instantly and so I am going out on a limb here.

You can choose to begin believing God today and
actually stay there no matter what comes to you.

Here's how I think we should begin. You've seen similar cleansing steps before, but they bear repeating in this context of becoming free of bitterness:

1. Confess any tendency you have toward bitterness. Maybe it's just always been your nature to be bitter. Maybe you learned bitterness in your upbringing. Even a lifetime of patterns does not have to own your future. Our God is more than able to change your nature and your learned habits. If you aren't sure if you harbor bitterness, just ask people who live or work with you. They probably have a pretty clear picture of what you cannot see.

I realize that praying prayers of confession is difficult for many of us. Just come in humility. Come knowing that God is truly in love with you. Ask Him to remove every root of bitterness and every tendency to grow more such roots.

2. Receive God's cleansing forgiveness. Remember, forgiveness is for forgiveness. Forgiveness should make us grateful.

3. Relinquish the old desire to harbor bitterness. Some people call this surrender, a spiritual giving up. It feels like an emotional deep breath to me where I picture the anger and resentment being drained from my body and I am being filled with the fresh, life-giving breath of God. I realize this may sound a little hokey to you. But giving up the practice of bitterness is a conscious act of your will. Paul said, "Get rid of all bitterness" (Ephesians 4:31 NIV). It is difficult for us, but God gives us the power to do what He has asked us to do.

4. Reject Satan's lies. He continues to be the deceiver. He whispers that you will find comfort in bitterness.

5. Apply God's grace to the people and circumstances in your life. I've had women tell me this feels impossible to them. I hear you. But this is where you take a step of maturity by faith or you remain locked inside the bitter jail. Forgive as you have been forgiven. Choosing to lay aside your judgment. Trusting God for your future and for His better will. Allowing others to prosper. Waiting for God. Each act of maturity requires grace. And God will give every grace you need to grow.

> *See to it that no one misses the grace of God and that*
> *no bitter root grows up to cause trouble and defile many.*
>
> (Hebrews 12:15 NIV)

6. Believe God. Here's what I know to be true: God really does have a plan and a purpose and a future for each one of us. He is sovereign and fully in control. He provides a way out and a way up. He redeems suffering and disciplines us from His Father-heart. He still loves broken people and He mends their brokenness.

We have a certain hope because we belong to God. Believing in that hope, no matter what, can wipe away every inclination we have toward bitterness. Halfhearted believing keeps us tripping along through the faith. Lean in. Put all your weight on the promises of God. Live the Bible without reservation, and watch the God of your hope show up.

> *God does not waste suffering, nor does He discipline out of caprice. If He plows, it is because He purposes a crop.*
>
> —J. Oswald Sanders

7. Start over at confession every time you need to until bitterness has no hold. Being a human is frustrating. I want to choose and then have it done forever. But my humanity keeps me on my knees asking again and again to be free. My imperfection keeps me fully dependent on the grace of God. For me, staying free means staying in the presence of God. And in the presence of God, bitterness will lose its attraction. The taste of it will eventually become repulsive and childish to you.

Choose Wisdom

Through the years, I have often prayed and asked God to make me wise. I don't think I realized what a big deal this was going to be or how much wisdom comes to us through pain and discipline. God lays before us the path of wisdom, but we have to choose it for ourselves. Foolishness comes so easily and is often the natural consequence of not choosing wisely.

Every morning during the school year, my clock goes off at 5:45 a.m. I have had a child in school for ten years, and I'm still not over having to wake up so early. Almost every day I lie there for the eight snooze minutes and tell myself, *You have to be the grown-up. No one is going to get the children up and ready for school unless you do it. Get up, Angela. Be a big girl. Come on.*

Getting everybody up, fed, and off to school is my responsibility. It goes along with being a parent and a grown-up. But I still have to tell myself to do it. I still have to choose every morning to be responsible and mature. I believe it's much the same way with wisdom.

Wisdom can be just down the hall waiting for us, but we can lie in the bed and keep hitting the snooze that calls us awake. It's just easier not to kick off the covers of our foolishness. It takes effort to throw our feet over the side of the bed and make our way toward right living. Choosing wisdom means that you are deciding to be a big girl and act like a big girl even when the little girl inside you wants to stay in bed.

It's the foolish little girl inside us who wants to hold on to bitterness. The whole book of Proverbs teaches us over and over—choose wisdom and you will receive blessing; choose foolishness and suffer the consequences.

> *My child, hold on to wisdom and good sense. Don't let them out of your sight.*
>
> They will give you life and beauty *like a necklace around your neck.*
>
> *Then you will go your way in safety, and you will not get hurt.*
>
> *When you lie down, you won't be afraid; when you lie down, you will sleep in peace.*
>
> *You won't be afraid of sudden trouble; you won't fear the ruin that comes to the wicked, because the LORD will keep you safe.*
>
> *He will keep you from being trapped.*
>
> (Proverbs 3:21–26 NCV, emphasis mine)

As you begin to resist bitterness and choose wisdom, God promises His blessing and protection.

I've met plenty of grown-up women who have lived their whole lives bitter and resentful. Not one of them would ever be regarded as wise. Childish? Yes. Immature? You betcha. Wise woman of God? No way.

We should take the apostle Paul's words from the Bible and make them our own:

> When I was a child, I talked like a child, I thought like a child, I reasoned like a child. When I became a [woman], I stopped those childish ways.
>
> (1 Corinthians 13:11 NCV)

Confident women believe in God. They choose wisdom and resist the childish ways of bitterness.

Choose Victory

There is a story about a woman who came to church for the very first time in her life. She heard the truth about Jesus that day and came to the front of the church to meet with the pastor. They talked for a while and the woman decided to trust Jesus as her Savior. The pastor wanted to meet with the woman in a week, but told her in the meantime she should get a Bible and begin reading.

The next day the brand-new believer came running into the pastor's office. "Preacher, I bought a Bible like you said and I've been reading it all day. I couldn't wait a week. I just had to come talk to you."

Curious about what was so urgent, the pastor asked, "What did you read?"

"Well, I didn't know where to begin, so when it flipped open to the book of Revelation I started there."

The pastor felt a little uneasy. This woman, who had never been to church in her life, began reading the Bible in one of the most difficult books to understand. "What did you learn?" the pastor hesitantly inquired.

"We win!" the woman exclaimed. "At the end, we win!"

The pastor smiled at the woman's understanding. "You're exactly right. We do win."

Maybe it hasn't been at the forefront of your thoughts lately, but we do win. The victory belongs to God. Evil will be punished. Righteousness will be rewarded. Every knee will bow before the King of heaven and earth. This train really is bound for glory.

You can choose this day to live your life in light of the victory that is promised. When a woman begins to live in the assurance of certain victory, then holding on to bitterness loses its power.

One day every tear will be wiped away. You will understand the purpose for every trial you have faced and the suffering you have known.

- You will no longer see through the mirror dimly.
- Satan is doomed. Evil will be bound and punished for eternity.
- You will enter into the promise of a new heaven and a new earth forever.
- You will finally be as God has always dreamed you would be.
- Victory belongs to everyone who calls Jesus Lord.

Read what John wrote to us in 1 John:

> *God's commands are not too hard for us, because*
> *everyone who is a child of God conquers the world. And*
> *this is the victory that conquers the world—our faith. So*
> *the one who wins against the world is the person who*
> *believes that Jesus is the Son of God.*
>
> (1 John 5:3–5 NCV)

How would things begin to change in your life if you began choosing to live in the victory that's already certain? I think if we believe God and keep heaven in view, so much that invites us to bitterness would fall away.

- You would not have to vie for position. Your place with God is certain.
- You could lay aside your judgment. God is the final judge.
- You could look forward to new adventure instead of back at every failure.
- Getting even would mean nothing. Getting right with God would mean everything.

In view of eternity and the victory that is sure, we can choose to become grown-up Jesus women. We can hear the Holy Spirit call and choose to get up and face our battles with courage instead of bitter hearts.

A few weeks ago I was teaching at a women's conference. It wasn't a part of what I'd planned to say, but for some reason I went down this path:

> *I am a single mom. I have four kids that I provide*
> *for. I am not dating. There is no one to catch me except*
> *Jesus. Life hasn't really turned out right, but Jesus is my*
> *Lord, and I am not bitter.*

The women burst into applause and began to stand. Their enthusiasm shocked me at first. They were cheering the decision to believe God instead of living bitter. Maybe it would help if you knew all of heaven does the same. Every time you believe God and resist bitterness, I'm sure the angels stand to applaud.

And every time you resist bitterness, that keeps God from having to stop the car, pull you over to the side of the road, and give you the *look-at-your-life-and-be-grateful-for-the-crackers-you-have* sermon.

a dancing lesson

The bitter wallflower focuses
only on the life she's never
known and the parties she
missed. The woman who
resists bitterness and
believes God is finally
ready to dance.

HE WORKS WHERE He sends us to wait.
—*Oswald Chambers*[1]

WAITING ON GOD is giving back to the
Father what He wants.
—*Mark Pate*

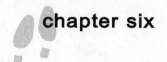

chapter six

Until It's Your Turn

L
ong before personal computers and online registration, people stood in line. At the University of North Carolina we stood in line for everything—precious parking stickers, class schedules, meal tickets, and any other commodity essential to collegiate life. After a while, you'd just walk past a long line and assume that you were probably supposed to be in it. The lines wound around buildings and across the quad, and the people you were waiting to see never got in a hurry. It could take all day just to drop a class, and the lines required to change a major, well, it was just easier to graduate with the one you started with.

But there was a crème de la crème of collegiate waiting. It was the camp-out-on-the-sidewalk, miss-all-your-classes line for basketball tickets. If there was ever a team worth sleeping outside on the concrete for, it was Michael Jordan and the Tarheels. During basketball season, thousands of us spent about one night a week bundled inside sleeping bags, camped out in a line that wrapped around the gym. We thought it was a blast, but even more than that, it was mandatory for a real fan. The kids who didn't wait all night didn't get tickets.

Funny thing about standing in line—maybe even more than actu-ally getting your turn—just knowing that you are *next* is a really great feeling.

Life can be a whole lot like standing in line. You get all your stuff together. Pack a snack. Choose the appropriate path. Muster up your patience. Square your determination. And wait to be next.

There is a great lesson that comes to those who have spent the good part of a lifetime waiting. Sometimes you have all your papers and the necessary credentials, you are in exactly the right line at exactly the right time, but you still have to wait. An agonizing wait. An I-wonder-if-I'm-in-the-right-line wait. A much longer wait than you had expected. All the time, you may be in the right place, facing the right direction, but it's just not your turn yet.

Not Yet

The mature woman knows how to wait on God. She has learned through tears, disappointments, and even rejection that sometimes it's just not your turn. That doesn't mean it won't ever be. Or that you're not qualified. Or that you've gone completely the wrong way. It's just not yet. John Piper wrote:

> *We are like farmers. They plow the field and plant the seed and cut away weeds and scare away crows, but they do not make the crop grow. God does. He sends rain and sunshine and brings to maturity the hidden life of the seed. We have our part. But it is not coercive or con-trolling. And there will be times when the crops fail. Even then God has his ways of feeding the farmer and*

bringing him through a lean season. We must learn to
wait for the Lord.[2]

To do everything we can, stay the course, and wait to be next requires a grown-up Jesus woman who has put away whining and manipulation. She has decided not to stomp her feet, huff and puff, groan and complain. She is waiting with integrity. Not cutting in line with her friend who's farther ahead. Not cheating for advantage. Not bargaining or bribing. Just waiting until she is called.

Maybe this lesson of *Not Yet* continues to be the one that most profoundly shapes my character and my heart. You really have to trust God to wait. You must believe in His divine love. You must lean into His arms and stop fidgeting with your own agenda. You must surrender your five-year plan and give up your pride. Waiting requires so much maturity that I understand why most of us just get out of line. Abandoning what we've been made for because the wait seemed too long.

Almost every arena of life requires a wait that is beyond my own ability. My professional career demands that I wait for approval. It mandates a public testing that will confirm or refute my readiness to go forward. The Lord beckons me to keep my eyes on Him, continue to walk in my calling, and understand that sometimes it's just not my turn.

Wait on God and He will work, but don't wait in
spiritual sulks because you cannot see an inch in front of
you!

—Oswald Chambers[3]

My mothering waits for fruit. Will all these years sow character in the ones I love? I see glimpses. I hope for more. Holding my breath. Praying my guts out. Waiting for the seeds and planting and pruning to grow into godly, faithful lives.

My heart waits to be loved by a man. It is an almost unceasing ache too painful to describe. Night after night of lonely integrity. Week after week of single mom in a family church. Another Valentine's Day bouquet from my sweet dad. Going on. Making plans. Buying a house. Putting up the Christmas tree. Alone. Trusting God. Waiting for my turn.

In each place I hear the Holy Spirit whisper, *Stay in line. Do not rush ahead of God. Stand with your head up. Stand with honor. Soon, it will be your turn.*

Where does life require you to wait? Some of my close friends wait for an adoption agency in China to tell them they can come for their daughter. Another friend waits for a degree she wishes she'd gotten twenty years ago. My high school girlfriend is waiting for ten more chemo treatments, a double mastectomy, and radiation to be completed. As this mother of two waits for restored health, each of her days is graciously teaching the rest of us about courage and complete dependence.

What to Do Until It's Your Turn

So how, then, shall we wait? If spiritual maturity is our goal and the fullness of the Holy Spirit is our desire, then how shall we wait before God? Waiting is not whining or fretting or looking over to compare whose turn came before ours. Waiting is an opportunity to grow up. To wait upon the Lord means choosing a higher road that most are not willing to take. Sometimes the wallflower has to wait to dance.

The big baby inside me is about three years old, and she wants to stomp her feet and scream for attention. She doesn't want to wait her turn. She wants to rush ahead to the front. She wants all the people who've ever pushed her aside to be pushed back. And she desperately wants to pout. When one of my kids pouts, I turn my head and smile, but when I meet a grown-up woman who pouts, I want to turn my head and roll my eyes.

God help us all from giving in to the baby girl. It's time to put away her childish behavior. Until it's your turn, which, by the way, seems to come so much more slowly for the whiners, there is an opportunity to choose the better way of maturity and spiritual growth. A long time ago I heard the adage *You haven't begun to wait until you think you've waited long enough.* By the time we're thirty-five, most of us feel we could write "Enough waiting, already" across all the pages in our journals. But maybe it's not about the length of time you have been waiting; maybe what matters more is *how*.

God gives us many desires that require a determined wait. The longing for romantic love. The desire to improve and use our gifts. A home that becomes a haven for family and friends. A strong physical body. The blessing of children. But the journey of desire is not a rocket ride. It's a spiritual marathon and, maybe even more than the desire itself, what matters is how you run toward it.

The following principles can help us wait in strength for our desires. As you take inventory of your waiting, whether spiritual, emotional, or physical, decide that you will make adjustments where necessary. Determine that you'll do whatever it takes to implement these directives. Sometimes it's just not your turn, but God wants to do amazing things in your life in the meantime.

1. Abide. Until it's your turn, God is asking you to stay with Him. Don't go anywhere. Remain. Stay. He wants you in His presence, moment by moment, so that step-by-step you hear His voice and turn at His will. Here's where most of us give up. The wait feels too long, so we assume God doesn't care. We push away from His presence to hurry things up.

In John 15, Jesus is giving the Upper Room instructions to His disciples. On this evening before His betrayal and arrest, He tells His followers that in the coming days they will need to remain with Him. Abide. Stay put. Wait. He is so concerned that they understand the importance of abiding that in ten verses, He tells them eleven times to *remain.* Those instructions continue with great relevance for our lives. While you are waiting—as you go, in season and out of season—you are called to remain with God.

> *Remain in me.*
> —Jesus, John 15:4 NCV

I love the writings of Andrew Murray. He knew so very much about the grace of God. For those of us who view abiding as another thing we have to figure out how to do, he wrote:

> *Abiding in Christ is just meant for the weak, and so beautifully suited to their feebleness. It is not the doing of some great thing, and does not demand that we first*

lead a very holy and devoted life. No, it is simply weakness entrusting itself to a Mighty One to be kept—the unfaithful one casting self on One who is altogether trustworthy and true. Abiding in Him is not a work that we have to do as the condition for enjoying His salvation, but a consenting to let Him do all for us, and in us, and through us. It is a work He does for us.[4]

Arriving at our destination gives new energy. A surge of enthusiasm and resolve to push across the finish line. Enough spiritual adrenaline to keep going.

But waiting. Waiting is so draining. We begin to stumble and lose focus and doubt. I love that the abiding Murray wrote about is for the weak. A tired woman like you or me. We can do that. We can lean in and ask God to take hold of us. To abide is to consent in your mind and in your spirit to give yourself to God for His keeping. Here is where you can be assured, the wallflower can fall into the strong arms of God and agree to stay there. He is the One who will lift you up to dance at exactly the right time.

2. Entrust. If I had something valuable that needed to be kept safe, let's say an antique vase, there's no way I'd entrust it to one of my children. They might intend to take care of it, but before you knew it, that heirloom would be full of kid treasures like gel pens and sticky candy, complete with glow-in-the-dark slime at the bottom. Nope, if I wanted my vase taken care of, I'd give it to my friend Lisa. The next time I needed it, I'm sure she'd know exactly where it was, right in the bin labeled *Keep for Angela*, bubble-wrapped and packed into a sturdy crate. I can be sure that anything I entrust to Lisa will come back better than I gave it to her. She's just that kind of organized, thoughtful, meticulous friend.

If Lisa would be careful with my vase, can you imagine how much more vigilant God will be with your heart's desire? He is both the Creator and the Master Planner. He is the Giver of your desires. You are a dreaming and becoming woman because you have been made that way. You are full of life and full of the desire for more life. You can entrust to God your heart, every need and every longing. As a matter of fact, you can begin to trust Him so much that your waiting becomes a beautiful offering. An act of devotion. A sacrifice of praise.

Not many months ago I was away speaking to a large group of women at a retreat center. In between the sessions I met privately with several different women for conversation or prayer. That weekend, there was one particular struggle that just kept coming up. Several of the women, all unknown to one another, were involved in extramarital affairs or were actively considering having an affair. I always assume that one brave woman speaks for about ten others, and so the weight of each new confession left me increasingly sad and heavyhearted.

During the last teaching session, as God would have it, I was speaking to the women about entrusting their hearts and dreams to Jesus. His great love. His capable hands. His understanding heart.

I hadn't planned to, but on that day I felt that I should share my own longings. I told them something like this:

You all know that I am a single mom. I'm forty-one. Some say that I'm in the prime of my life, and I'd have to agree. These years are very beautiful and exciting to me. But they are not without sadness or disappointment. There is a painful loneliness that can come to the feminine soul. We were made for romantic, intimate love and without it, the heart becomes weary and longing begins to magnify the emptiness.

I am not dating. I also don't have any sense that dating or marriage is in my near future. But I am just a woman, and I have all the same desires that come with being made feminine. So there are some days and nights when my longing becomes grieving.

Some well-meaning people have said to me, "God will be your husband." To which I wanted to reply, "You're a nerd," but I haven't. I realize people mean well and they want to give comfort, but they don't have words for what they haven't experienced or the emptiness they've long forgotten.

Here's what I know: God made me for the arms of a man. His design. His idea. He is very aware that my heart longs for romance and physical intimacy. He also knows that my *prime years* are skipping right by. And here is what I have said to God:

Father, I entrust to You my sexuality. I give You my heart of desire. I lay all my romantic dreams at Your feet. Paris in the fall, tropical island getaways. I speak to You in honesty and in righteousness. It's just me. The woman

You made. Entrusting my longings to the God I love.
Would You keep all the treasures of my heart safe until
Your appointed time? Would You return to me, with
multiplied joy, all the years that I wait? And God, if it
would be okay with You, I'd like to have sex with a lov-
ing husband before menopause.

Are you willing to entrust whatever is precious or desired to your
Father, who has promised to be faithful? The psalmist said:

> *People, trust God all the time. Tell him all your prob-*
> *lems, because God is our protection.*
>
> (Psalm 62:8 NCV)

I am believing with my whole life that while we wait, God can be
entrusted to protect and defend the treasures of the woman He loves.
I also believe that the act of entrusting is an act of submission. To
submit to God as Lord. To entrust and believe in His love with your
treasure.

3. Trust. We entrust our treasures for safekeeping and then we trust
the One to whom they have been given. I believe Brennan Manning explained trusting God best in this passage from his book
Ruthless Trust:

> *When the brilliant ethicist John Kavanaugh went*
> *to work for three months at "the house of dying" in*
> *Calcutta, he was seeking a clear answer as to how best*
> *to spend the rest of his life. On the first morning there*

he met Mother Teresa. She asked, "And what can I do for you?" Kavanaugh asked her to pray for him. "What do you want me to pray for?" she asked. He voiced the request that he had borne thousands of miles from the United States: "Pray that I have clarity."

She said firmly, "No, I will not do that." When he asked her why, she said, "Clarity is the last thing you are clinging to and must let go of." When Kavanaugh commented that she always seemed to have the clarity he longed for, she laughed and said, "I have never had clarity; what I have always had is trust. So I will pray that you trust God."

We ourselves have known and put our trust in God's love toward ourselves (1 John 4:16). Craving clarity, we attempt to eliminate the risk of trusting God. Fear of the unknown path stretching ahead of us destroys childlike trust in the Father's active goodness and unrestricted love.

We often presume that trust will dispel the confusion, illuminate the darkness, vanquish the uncertainty, and redeem the times. But the crowd of witnesses in Hebrews 11 testifies that this is not the case. Our trust does not bring final clarity on this earth. It does not still the chaos or dull the pain or provide a crutch. When all else is unclear, the heart of trust says, as Jesus did on the cross, "Into your hands I commit my spirit." (Luke 23:46)[5]

4. Become. When it's finally your turn, wouldn't it be devastating not to be ready? God would say, "Next." And you'd say, "Can I get a few more minutes? I'm not quite there yet." In this season of waiting, you and I are responsible for becoming ready, preparing to step up when we're called. Being shaped into the women God wants to use.

Sometimes after an event a woman will come to me and tell me she wants to do what I do. She would like to write books and speak to women. Then she'll graciously ask me for some pointers. I almost hate those hopeful questions, because I know that I'm getting ready to give her an answer she doesn't want to hear.

Twenty years ago, I knew that I wanted to do this too. I went to seminary to get ready. Then I went on staff at a church where my training with people began in earnest. For the next fifteen years, I would teach anywhere anybody needed a woman like me to show up—the garden club, a last-minute replacement for the real speaker who missed her plane, or at some event where people were eating. For the record, it's very humbling to talk about anything—especially anything spiritual—while people are eating. They really don't care so much when there is food. I think all wannabe speakers should have to speak while there is food four or five times a year, just to keep perspective.

So I've been doing the same thing for about twenty years. Trying to teach the Bible in fresh, energetic ways that a woman can apply to her life. It's just that the venues have changed a little in the past few years.

Almost everywhere I go someone will say to me, "I had never heard of you before." I love that, because God has known me all along and all this time, under His watchful care, I have been quietly becoming and waiting for my turn. To this day I read everything I can get my hands on, listen to teaching CDs, and sleep with systematic theology books in stacks beside my bed. A total geek.

Always learning. Still getting ready. Waiting for God to show me what's next.

While you wait, are you actively becoming the woman God can use? Are you faithful to prepare? I realize your life is busy, but when there is an hour, or half a day, what do you do with it? I want to encourage you to make some life priorities and then spend any extra time you have focused on practical ways to become the woman you've dreamed of.

One day, you'll be next. If you're ready, it will be the thrill of a lifetime to step up for your turn in confidence. When God calls your name, you want to be ready to dance.

5. Pray. Andrew Murray wrote:

> We must . . . wait on God in prayer. [The disciples] waited, they prayed with one accord; prayer and supplication went up to God mingled with praise. They expected—our primary lesson—God in heaven to do something. I wish I could stress the importance of that! I find believers—and I have found in my own experience—who read, and understand, and think, and wish, and want to claim, and want to take, and want to get, and yet what they desire eludes their grasp. Why? Because they do not wait for God to give it.[6]

Prayer is the means by which we continually place ourselves into the arms of God. When you meet a woman who is full of joy and confidence no matter what her circumstances, you have most likely encountered a woman of prayer.

> *If one labors to come into the presence of God, then men and women will respond to the presence of God in you.*
>
> —Mark Pate

I have the most vivid memories of a woman from the church I grew up in. Her countenance was genuinely peaceful. Her home was open and warm and inviting. We kids never felt the pressure to keep a lot of rules when we were with her, but that only made us want to please her more. After I was grown and moved away, I came to know this childhood neighbor as a woman of prayer. That one characteristic made everything else about her make sense to me. Of course she prayed; everything we knew about her had been shaped by the years of consistent praying.

Prayer is the discipline by which God gives us the ability to wait. To persevere. To dream again. And to trust.

6. Stand. Two weeks ago my group of eight girlfriends met for a birthday lunch. We get together as often as possible, especially if gifts and food are involved. A local restaurant had a back room that we could pile into and, amazingly, all of us were there. It almost seems statistically impossible, but each one of these women is a stay-at-home mom and very happily married. I am the only weird single mom in the bunch, and I'm very grateful they let me hang around.

What that means is these friends have walked through so much with me the past years. So much, in fact, that their arms should be tired of carrying me. This particular lunch was festive and fun. We hadn't all been together in too long. There was so much to catch up on. Just as everyone was about to leave, I had to totally bring the whole party down. I had been facing unrelenting attack in the past weeks, and I was emotionally and spiritually exhausted. I felt God prompting me to ask for prayer. *These are your friends. Ask them to pray for you.* And so I did.

The minute they heard my voice quiver, these women moved from all around the table to touch me or hold me. *Single* means you don't get held so much. I really needed to be held. Each one began to pray for me and over me. My friend Jamie took my hands and said, "Angela, stand up."

Right in the middle of our back room at the Greek restaurant, decorated with party streamers and jumbled with little bags of gifts, I stood up, completely awash in tears. Sobbing. My girlfriends all stood around me. Then Jamie began to quote this passage and pray it for me:

> *Therefore put on the full armor of God, so that when the day of evil comes, you may be able to stand your ground,* and after you have done everything, to stand.
> (Ephesians 6:13 NIV, emphasis mine)

Sometimes you have done everything you know to do. You abide in Christ and long for His presence. You entrust everything and everybody and keep entrusting day after day. You are faithful to become and change and to seek wisdom and growth. You pray. So all that is left, after you have done everything, is to stand. Maybe you can't take one more step. Just stand. Maybe you're tired of the wait. Keep standing. Maybe it seems it will never be your turn. Stand.

The physical act of standing up in that restaurant left me trembling. Jamie took hold of my hands with authority. She lovingly looked into my eyes. And then she instructed me, according to the admonition of Scripture, to stand. As an act of obedience to God, as a sign of my determined faith, there was nothing else to do except stand.

Maybe today you don't know what else to do. You are tired and can't go forward. You have considered just getting out of line and abandoning the wait. Can I ask you to do something? If you are able in this moment, stand up. Physically stand up and pray:

> *God, I cannot see You. I have no idea what to do next. But as an act of my complete trust, I will stand and keep standing until You show me what to do. Amen.*

One of my favorite stories in Scripture is in the book of 2 Chronicles. Jehoshaphat is a man of God. He sought the Lord for direction. He led as he believed God had instructed. But after all those things, Jehoshaphat and his people found themselves under attack from a vast army. The Bible says that when they saw the army coming with no power to protect themselves, Jehoshaphat cried out to the Lord,

> *We do not know what to do, but* our eyes are upon you.

> (20:12 NIV, emphasis mine)

The Scripture says that then

> *all the men of Judah, with their wives and children*
> *and little ones,* stood there before the LORD.
>
> (v. 13, emphasis mine)

I love that. What great courage comes to us through their vulnerability and act of obedience. When the people of Judah did not know what to do, they kept their eyes on God and stood. This story just gets better, and you have to hear what happens after the people stood before their Lord. God began to speak through a man named Jahaziel. He told them:

> *Listen, King Jehoshaphat and all who live in Judah*
> *and Jerusalem! This is what the LORD says to you: "Do*
> *not be afraid or discouraged because of this vast army.*
> *For the battle is not yours, but God's . . . You will not*
> *have to fight this battle. Take up your positions;* stand
> firm and see the deliverance the LORD will give you,
> *O Judah and Jerusalem. Do not be afraid; do not be dis-*
> *couraged. Go out to face them tomorrow, and the LORD*
> *will be with you."*
>
> *Jehoshaphat bowed with his face to the ground, and*
> *all the people of Judah and Jerusalem fell down in wor-*
> *ship before the LORD.*
>
> (vv. 15, 17–18 NIV, emphasis mine)

Early the next morning the king and his men went out to face the army. Jehoshaphat appointed men to go before them singing praises to God. Then as they began to sing, the Lord set ambushes against the invading army and they were defeated.

> *When the men of Judah came to the place that overlooks the desert and looked toward the vast army, they saw only dead bodies lying on the ground; no one had escaped . . . Then, led by Jehoshaphat, all the men of Judah and Jerusalem returned joyfully to Jerusalem, for the LORD had given them cause to rejoice over their enemies.*
>
> (vv. 24, 27 NIV)

There are many opposing armies in the life of a woman. Lies we believe. Difficult relationships. Financial hardship. Whatever battle you face this day, it cannot have you. You belong to God. After you have done everything you can do, then stand and wait to see the glory of the Lord.

Wait on the Lord. Until it's your turn, I want you to become aware of God's intimate presence in your waiting. He is not far away. He is here. Holding you. I want you to know His pleasure. He is perfecting all those things that concern you.

God can give you a righteous confidence in your waiting. And when it's finally your turn and He says, "Next," what a thrill it will be to yell, "Hey, that's me! I'm ready to dance!"

a dancing lesson

Sometimes the wallflower has
to get ready, get to the
ballroom, and then
patiently wait for her
turn to dance.

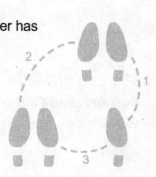

THE ONE AND ONLY characteristic of the Holy Ghost in a man is a strong family likeness to Jesus Christ, and freedom from everything that is unlike Him.

—*Oswald Chambers* [1]

GOD GIVES HIS authority to friends and lovers, not the casual observer.

—*Mark Pate*

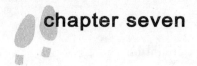

chapter seven

The Filling of the Holy Spirit

There is a difference in the woman who is saved and getting by as best she can and the woman who is saved and living every day of her life filled by the power of the Holy Spirit. The first woman is a carnal Christian. And the second one is a spiritual woman. If we stay with our illustration, we'd say that the second woman is dancing. The first one continues to walk according to her old desires, and the other is being led by the Spirit of God. There is only one degree of choosing that separates these women. But as it turns out, one degree makes all the difference.

When you are saved, several things happen. The Holy Spirit has opened your heart to pay attention and receive the Word of God (Acts 16:14). God has called you and drawn you to believe in His Son, Jesus Christ (1 Corinthians 1:24; John 6:44). The Holy Spirit has crucified the old sinful self (Galatians 5:24) and taken away the power of sin (Romans 6:6). Through repentance, the woman who is saved turns to Christ as her Savior and begins the process of setting aside the sins that have plagued her life. At the beginning of our life in Christ, we are spiritual babies.

Remember Paul's words to the Corinthians:

> *Brothers and sisters, in the past I could not talk to you as I talk to spiritual people. I had to talk to you as I would to people without the Spirit—babies in Christ. The teaching I gave you was like milk, not solid food, because you were not able to take solid food. And even now you are not ready. You are still not spiritual, because there is jealousy and quarreling among you, and this shows that you are not spiritual. You are acting like people of the world.*
>
> (1 Corinthians 3:1–3 NCV)

We begin as babies, and it's important for us to remember that God has great patience with new believers. He understands the weakness by which we begin. Just learning about grace. Only beginning to walk by faith and battle our old sin patterns. The very good news is that there is hope for those of us who struggle in earnest to become women of great faith. There is a place in Christ for the stragglers and beginners and stumblers.

Brennan Manning talks about the way we come to Christ so beautifully in his introduction to one of my all-time favorite books, *The Ragamuffin Gospel.* In this book, he presents the gospel of Jesus as a gospel of grace and freedom. His teaching has radically shaped my heart, my own understanding of God's mind-boggling love for me, and my compassion for others. In his introduction Brennan talks about who his book is written for. Ultimately, he is speaking about the gospel of Christ and who is offered the grace and mercy of our Savior.

[It is] for the bedraggled, beat-up, and burnt-out.

It is for the sorely burdened who are still shifting the heavy suitcase from one hand to the other.

It is for the wobbly and weak-kneed who know they don't have it altogether and are too proud to accept the handout of amazing grace.

It is for inconsistent, unsteady disciples whose cheese is falling off their cracker.

It is for poor, weak, sinful men and women with hereditary faults and limited talents.

It is for earthen vessels who shuffle along on feet of clay.

It is for the bent and bruised who feel that their lives are a grave disappointment to God.

It is for smart people who know they are stupid and honest disciples who admit they are scalawags.[2]

We all come to Jesus as ragamuffins. And many times we find ourselves back at ragamuffin again. Thankfully, none are ever turned away from the grace of God. All of us have a certain hope because of God's patient mercy and love.

But Scripture says that even though we come to Christ as ragamuffins and live a lifetime as just women covered by grace, from our gratitude for God's magnificent grace to us, we are called to grow up in His mercy. To graduate from baby milk to solid food.

But becoming a mature, spiritual woman requires the next step of choosing. That one degree of difference is the way of becoming a woman of righteous confidence. The woman who is becoming spiritual is being filled and refilled by the powerful presence of the Holy

Spirit. The abundant, full life that Christ promises in John 10:10 comes to us from the full indwelling of the Holy Spirit in us.

> *I came to give life—life in all its fullness.*
> —Jesus, John 10:10 NCV

I spent much of my life as a believer not understanding the importance of the Holy Spirit in me and through me. So I don't mean to make this too simplistic. I don't want to insult your intelligence or make any assumptions. It's just that many women do not live in this fullness. If I could take you by the hand and, according to Scripture, walk you step-by-step toward understanding the gift of the Holy Spirit, here's the way I believe we should begin.

Stepping Into

The way out of un-woman and into maturity is the step from carnal living over into a spiritual life of growth and becoming. Spiritual maturity is a gradual process by which Christ in us begins to subdue our old sin nature and we become more in tune to the Holy Spirit. The fruit of the Holy Spirit becomes more and more evident in our lives as we grow spiritually. Old sins lose their hold. And all this comes to pass as we learn to trust Christ more fully as our daily guide and real friend. Believing that Jesus is for us and learning to live out of that kind of love. This process of maturing happens as we step over into the work of the Holy Spirit.

The first question for us is this: Have you made a conscious decision to step from a carnal life into a spiritual life? Remember, there is one degree of choosing that separates the carnal from the spiritual. Both are saved, one living in power and one not. Before we go any further, stop and consider your own choosing. Have you decided to pursue a spiritual life? Have you consciously made the decision to surrender your heart and your life for the filling of the Holy Spirit? On this day, do you need to recommit to a fresh start? Remember, we will go forward by prayer.

Your Father so very much wants you to live in power and confidence. He waits to give all that you need. Would you step over today and give your heart fully to the process of growing and becoming a confident woman by the power of the Holy Spirit?

Without Fear

I have girlfriends who tell me that talking about the Holy Spirit makes them nervous. They're afraid that just as soon as we begin studying the work of the Holy Spirit, somehow, it's going to get hokey, someone will say something about praying in tongues, objects will begin floating around the room, then they'll feel anxious and give up considering the fullness of the Spirit once again.

To every woman who has ever been misinformed about the indwelling of God through His Spirit, I apologize.

What I want you to see is that the indwelling of the Holy Spirit is to be desired. He is the promised Comforter. He is the pledge of God's commitment to work through us. His sustained presence brings the fullness of spiritual gifts that we long for. The woman who is spiritual is the woman who has come to be filled and refilled by God's Holy Spirit.

Every gift from the Father is good. We do not have to be afraid of His work in us or hesitate about becoming *filled with the Spirit.*

When the Spirit Lives Inside You

Do you remember the disciples after they had been called by Jesus? Their next three years were spent with Him as God in the flesh and yet Jesus lived outside their bodies. They walked with Him, ate with Him, and witnessed His miracles with their own eyes. But Jesus did not yet live inside them. What we remember about the disciples during those days is their weakness, their lack of confidence, and their struggle with pride. Many times, they gave up on the Savior, denied Him, fell asleep on Him, and fought over who would be the greatest in His kingdom.

But the night before His betrayal, Jesus promised the disciples that the Holy Spirit would come after Him to live inside them and give them power. That same promise holds for every believer today.

> *I will ask the Father, and he will give you another Helper to be with you forever—the Spirit of truth. The world cannot accept him, because it does not see him or know him. But you know him, because he lives with you and he will be in you.*
>
> (John 14:16–17 NCV)

> *If people love me, they will obey my teaching. My Father will love them, and we will come to them [through the Holy Spirit] and make our home with them.*
>
> (John 14:23 NCV)

> *But the Helper will teach you everything and will cause you to remember all that I told you. This Helper*

is the Holy Spirit whom the Father will send in my
name. I leave you peace; my peace I give you. I do not
give it to you as the world does. So don't let your hearts
be troubled or afraid.

(John 14:26–27 NCV)

Jesus' final words of instruction to the disciples just before He ascended into heaven were:

Wait here to receive the promise from the Father
which I told you about . . . When the Holy Spirit comes
to you, you will receive power.

(Acts 1:4, 8 NCV)

On the Day of Pentecost, the promised Helper called the Holy Spirit came to live inside the disciples.

They were all filled with the Holy Spirit.

(Acts 2:4 NCV)

After this day, when the promised indwelling of God was given to the believers, the rest of Scripture testifies to the radical difference this new power made in the hearts and lives of the disciples.

- The light of Christ came into the darkness of their hearts. Where the light filled, darkness was removed. Though still completely human, this light of God inside them made them holy.

- The timid and fearful disciples, once consumed
  with pride, became humble servants who were bold
  enough to speak even though threatened with death.
  Their works changed. They spoke with confidence.
  Their hearts broke with compassion for the lost and
  the suffering.
- The Holy Spirit changed the disciples' relationships
  with one another. His indwelling love began to unite
  them as one body. They put off bickering and
  selfishness. They began to sell their possessions to care
  for one another. They welcomed strangers whom they
  had begun to see with their new eyes. They
  understood their place in God's calling with a new
  heart of compassion and resolve.

I don't know about you, but too many times I have been a whimpering, fearful disciple, obviously not operating in the fullness of the Holy Spirit. More than anything, I want every facet of my life to be radically changed and impacted by the same anointing and indwelling the disciples received.

Can you imagine what kind of women we would be if every act and attitude were formulated from the depths of God's Fatherheart? Do you realize how significant this kind of spiritual abundance could be to every relationship and circumstance we navigate?

We can look at the lives of the disciples and be absolutely sure of it. We will never become women of righteous confidence apart from the fullness of the Holy Spirit.

Will you pursue God with me? Will you persist in prayer? I want to be filled to the measure of all fullness by the living, powerful presence of the Holy Spirit. Oh, Jesus, come and make it so for each of us.

How?

Certainly, the most prominent question in this pursuit begins to be *How?* How do I give myself to the process of filling? What is my part in being filled by the Holy Spirit? Is filling something that continues to happen unconsciously after I become a believer or do I have a role?

As we look to Scripture to answer the question of *How?* let's first consider some of the building blocks of truth about the Holy Spirit.

- The Holy Spirit comes to live inside the person who has accepted Jesus as Savior.

> *Peter said to them, "Change your hearts and lives and be baptized, each one of you, in the name of Jesus Christ for the forgiveness of your sins. And you will receive the gift of the Holy Spirit. This promise is for you, for your children, and for all who are far away. It is for everyone the Lord our God calls to himself."*
>
> (Acts 2:38–39 NCV)

- The Holy Spirit exists to mediate our relationship with Jesus, to make Christ real to people and bring glory to God.

> *The Spirit of truth will bring glory to me.*
> —Jesus, John 16:14 NCV

- The Holy Spirit is free to come and go as He pleases.
  He acts according to His will.

> *God also testified to it by signs, wonders and various*
> *miracles, and gifts of the Holy Spirit distributed* accord-
> ing to his will.
>
> (Hebrews 2:4 NIV, emphasis mine)

We cannot manipulate the presence of the Holy Spirit. He comes
to us at first as a gift and then more fully according to His own will.
Jesus says the Holy Spirit is as free as the wind (John 3:8). He cannot be seen or controlled. He goes where He pleases. He is free.

So now what? If the Holy Spirit is free to go wherever He pleases
and He moves only at His own will, then what do we possibly have
to do with the pursuit of His presence in our lives? How does a
woman seek the fullness of the Holy Spirit in her everyday heart and
her everyday life? The testimony of the Holy Spirit in Scripture gives
us more direction.

In Acts 10, Peter is preaching. The Bible tells us that before he is
finished, even before an invitation was given or the last hymn was
sung, the Holy Spirit came.

> *While Peter was still saying this, the* Holy Spirit
> came down *on all those who were listening.*
>
> (Acts 10:44 NCV, emphasis mine)

We just learned that the Holy Spirit has a free will. Peter could not
make Him "come down on" those who were listening that day. But

is there some correlation between what Peter was preaching or how he was preaching and the coming of the Spirit? I believe there is.

From the passage concerning Peter's preaching in Acts, we read that Peter was preaching many truths about Jesus. Jesus as the Peacemaker. Jesus as Lord of all. Jesus anointed with the Holy Spirit and power. Jesus stronger than sin and Satan. Jesus who was raised from the dead. Jesus the final Judge of every person. And Jesus as the forgiveness of sins. Do you remember that one of the purposes of the Holy Spirit is to glorify God?

From this passage, it seems that the Holy Spirit is more likely to come where the truth of Jesus is being clearly spoken. Where Jesus is being lifted up. Where we have made Jesus and His character the focus of our attention. The Holy Spirit is appointed to glorify the Son of God, and I believe He comes to give fullness to the life that has centered itself on Christ.

> *If I am lifted up from the earth, I will draw all people toward me.*
>
> —Jesus, John 12:32 NCV

At the Center of Your Life

I am praying that by this time, you are beginning to consider your life with the Lord. I am praying that you choose to intentionally step over from saved un-woman into the spiritual life of maturity and growth. The help that is necessary for each of us to step over, grow, and become is given to us through this powerful gift of the Holy Spirit. If we are to know Him more fully and operate in His power,

I believe our first priority is to take the story of Peter's teaching to heart and center our lives on Jesus.

I am a bit hesitant about the next thing I feel led to do. I want us to walk through the different areas of our lives in order to evaluate where we are and what needs to happen so that we live more Christ-centered. Here is my hesitation. You could misunderstand. Outlining these thoughts might begin to feel like a list of rules or things you have to be in order to manipulate the Holy Spirit. I'll say it again: all of Scripture testifies that the Spirit is free to work according to His will. We cannot make up rules to legislate His work. But our lives can make Him welcome and invite His sustained presence.

In a righteous pursuit of the presence of the Holy Spirit, I feel very strongly that we should examine the way we live and interact. The Spirit loves to glorify Christ. Does your life exalt Jesus? Does your countenance make Him welcome? Would the Spirit come and find a woman whose life is dedicated to her Father? A woman who walks in obedience? Let's begin on the inside and work our way out.

Your Mind

As you consider your thinking life, what do you find? A woman who longs for the Word of God? His guidance. His principles. His direction. Or a woman who has forgotten about the power of the Word to give life? Have you become a woman who thinks apart from the Spirit?

> *Those who live following their sinful selves think*
> *only about things that their sinful selves want. But*
> *those who live following the Spirit are thinking about*

*the things the Spirit wants them to do. If people's think-
ing is controlled by the sinful self, there is death. But if
their thinking is controlled by the Spirit, there is life
and peace.*

(Romans 8:5–6 NCV)

I realize that we live in a world where there is so much unavoidable
garbage coming into our minds. I also realize that you are a grown-up
who should be able to filter out what is inappropriate for a godly
woman to keep stored. But for the woman who is not intentionally
removing the evil, the garbage can really stack up fast. Consider what
you watch, maybe not once but repeatedly, again and again becoming
desensitized to its content. What do you read? Study? Meditate on?

Whom do you listen to? Who speaks the truths that shape your
thinking? How do you feed your mind? Where do you turn for
advice or counsel? How could you begin to exalt Jesus with your
thinking?

Your Countenance

If I were the Holy Spirit, and we're all certainly glad that I'm not,
there are some people I just wouldn't want to live inside of. Grumpy
people. Perpetually angry people. Vindictive people. A petulant,
sulky countenance is not very inviting to anyone and probably not to
the Holy Spirit as well.

I realize that we all have gloomy days and times of sadness, but if
the countenance is a reflection of the heart, what would yours usually reveal? How about your general disposition? Do people regard
you as negative? Angry? Pessimistic? Apathetic? Do you invite the

Holy Spirit to come and abide powerfully in your life through your countenance? Or do you imagine He'd want to avoid you?

Look at what the Spirit can do with your temperament:

> But the Spirit produces the fruit of love, joy, peace, patience, kindness, goodness, faithfulness, gentleness, self-control.
>
> (Galatians 5:22–23 NCV)

Would you make Him welcome in your life? Submit your countenance, humble your attitude, and lift up Jesus with your life so He can begin to produce the fruit that will transform your nature.

Your Home

You may think this is a bit over the edge, but I am fiercely protective of the things and people that come into my home. I am working really hard to create a haven of peace and respite for my family. I want this setting to be inviting to the Holy Spirit. I want my children to know what it feels like to live where the Spirit lives, and I want them to know the difference when they are apart from Him.

I have put copies of Scripture and references to the Word all through our home. I filter the television. None of the children have Internet privileges. No one can watch a movie at home or even away without permission. Where there is coarse talk, there are serious liquid soap consequences. Everyone knows I'll sit all their friends down and have a "Come to Jesus" meeting at the drop of a bad attitude. I want it to be fun here. I want them to dance here. I want Jesus to be exalted here.

The LORD is your protection; you have made God
Most High your place of safety. Nothing bad will hap-
pen to you; no disaster will come to your home. He has
put his angels in charge of you to watch over you wher-
ever you go.

(Psalm 91:9–11 NCV)

As you look around your home, what do you see? Invitations to walk in peace and holiness? Reminders of the love of God and His good gifts to you?

Do your surroundings invite the presence of the Holy Spirit or do they cultivate darkness and the presence of evil? I realize this may be misinterpreted as legalistic or small-minded, but I will not allow either the presence of evil or a representation of evil in our home. I'll do whatever is necessary to have it removed. We have enough to battle. Evil and its subtle incarnations are not welcome here.

Hate what is evil, and hold on to what is good.

(Romans 12:9 NCV)

Your Choices

Here's where I may really begin to get on your nerves, or step on your toes, or both. I believe I am supposed to speak boldly in these next ideas, but please hear my heart of grace in these thoughts.

As believers, we might read all the right things and think on the Word of God, seek Him in private prayer and in public worship. We can have a radiant countenance that perhaps just comes naturally. We may have a distinctly Christian home that valiantly proclaims our beliefs and rejects evil. We may even work in ministry or a Christian profession where all day, every day, is devoted to making Christ known. There are many people who live in just this way. And yet, many of these Christians are choosing poorly.

The Scripture is very clear in its call to live in obedience. Some things aren't even gray. The line is not blurry. No speculation is needed. I will be the very first in line to celebrate all the freedom that Christ has given to us. As a matter of fact, in most of my teaching I find myself working hard to set women free from the bondage they have known all in the name of religious rules and misapplication of Scripture. But today I want to speak to obedience in your choosing. If we desire to live in such a way as to make the Holy Spirit welcome, there are choices that really matter. Okay, buckle up.

• You cannot have sex outside marriage. Obvious, I realize, but it's amazing how many Christians disregard this very clear teaching, especially older singles. Seems like the young kids have been zealous in their commitment to wait. Many of us need to decide again that we will wait.

> *God wants you to be holy and to stay away from*
> *sexual sins. He wants each of you to learn to control*
> *your own body in a way that is holy and honorable.*
> *Don't use your body for sexual sin like the people who*
> *do not know God.*
>
> (1 Thessalonians 4:3–5 NCV)

• You cannot get drunk. Again, duh, this one is not some obscure, irrelevant Bible teaching. It's meant for us, the believers who want to pursue the heart of God. In case you missed it, really great Christians make very stupid choices when they are drunk.

> *Do not be drunk with wine, which will ruin you,*
> *but be filled with the Spirit.*
>
> (Ephesians 5:18 NCV)

• You cannot watch evil or invest your time in evil. Include here all forms of pornography, pornographic magazines, romance reading, and chat rooms that conduct lewd conversations. It's sick to me that hotels report their highest levels of pornographic viewing when they are hosting a pastors' conference. And women are not excluded from this category. What would the history page on your computer reveal? I realize you can be a lonely single or a lonely married woman, but you just cannot go here. Take up knitting. Go down to the homeless shelter and help somebody. Get help for yourself. Whatever it takes, because you cannot indulge your curiosity or the sickness any longer.

> *I will not look at anything wicked.*
>
> (Psalm 101:3 NCV)

• You cannot cheat or steal or covet. Again, a teaching that is so blatantly evident throughout Scripture. But Christians are cheating and wondering why there is no power in their lives. Work hard in the direction of your desires. But you cannot shortchange the process by cheating. There are devastating consequences for scoundrels.

> *You must not steal.*
>
> (Exodus 20:15 NCV)

- You cannot be lazy. Well, you can, and some believers are, but there are sad repercussions for your poor choosing.

> *How long will you lie there, you lazy person? When*
> *will you get up from sleeping? You sleep a little; you take*
> *a nap. You fold your hands and lie down to rest. So you*
> *will be as poor as if you had been robbed; you will have*
> *as little as if you had been held up.*
>
> (Proverbs 6:9–11 NCV)

Clearly, there is a very specific call to obedience in Scripture. Much of that obedience affects our personal and private choosing. I am only getting us started with these thoughts. But as much as Jesus offers His free grace and mercy to all of us, His call to obedience cannot be ignored. Obedience is living grateful for God's goodness. If you desire the presence of the Holy Spirit, I am very certain that He cannot come with fullness into a heart of willful disobedience.

In the next chapter I want us to continue understanding how vital the Holy Spirit is in our maturing and growth. When I meet a woman who is dancing with God, I am absolutely sure that she is dancing from the fullness of God's promised gift through the Holy Spirit.

a dancing lesson

Wallflowers are not only
invited to dance in the
arms of God; they are
given every ability
necessary by the fullness
of the Holy Spirit.

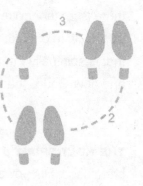

LIVING FROM OUR hearts is not simply doing what our feelings tell us. That would be folly. Living from our hearts means that there is an inner directive that, if governed by the Spirit of God, keeps us on a path that is spiritually attuned to who we are and how God is leading.[1]

THE HOLY SPIRIT'S power cannot be harnessed. His power cannot be used to accomplish anything other than the Father's will. He is not a candy dispenser. He is not a vending machine. He is not a genie waiting for someone to rub His lamp the right way. *He is holy God.*[2]

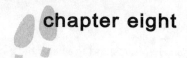

chapter eight

The Power of the Holy Spirit

When I was a little girl, I was raised in a house of faith, but I did not understand salvation. Every night as I went to bed, I would beg God to take me to heaven if I died in my sleep. Later, as I became older, I heard about "being saved," but it seemed extremist and outside my understanding of God. No one ever explained "being saved" to me, and I never pursued that foreign doctrine on my own. Still, I prayed every night and pleaded with God to save me from hell and allow me into heaven if I died while I slept. I'm not sure what I thought was going to happen if I kicked over during the day, but with the night my eternity always seemed more pressing.

Eventually, in college I really came to understand the idea of being saved. Not only did I begin to understand this new information, but what had once seemed outside my box, or outside what I had determined I needed, finally felt like exactly what I had been looking for all of my life. I prayed that very moment and asked Jesus to forgive me of my sins and save me for eternity with

Him in heaven. Still, I did not completely understand the heart of the Father. So I continued to pray that same prayer, asking God to save me, for the next five or six years.

Through discipleship I began to grow in both the knowledge of God's truth and its application for my life. I was both surprised and thankful to learn that I could be certain of my salvation. After I finally became sure of "being saved," I grew through the next years at a spiritual warp speed. My heart was a sponge and took in everything I could learn about Jesus. After a season of intense growth, I took all my newly obtained knowledge and, with great pleasure and a bit of arrogance, drew a different, bigger box around God. I decided everything that could be known about God was inside my box. It felt good to finally understand Him and own enough theology books to make me feel really smart about His character and His ways. Essentially, I thought I had God figured out, mostly.

One of the walls around my new box had to do with the Holy Spirit. As far as I knew, the Holy Spirit came to live inside you at salvation. He was God's presence and seal. He would intercede. He would comfort. He would convict and He would guide. I believed I would mature spiritually because the Holy Spirit would guide me into deeper knowledge and help me keep the walls of my spiritual box tight and secure. The Holy Spirit would keep out anything that did not fit neatly into my own personal systematic theology.

I knew of others who wanted the filling of the Holy Spirit, but for some reason I was satisfied with just the assurance of His presence. Being filled with the Holy Spirit was outside my information and outside my tradition. Pursuing knowledge and personal discipline was more in keeping with my training and my understanding.

Here's what I want you to get before I did: being completely filled with the Holy Spirit is desirable above all spiritual pursuits. Ordering your life around the pursuit of the Holy Spirit is the right order. From His fullness in you, every desire of God for you is free to be released and followed.

Maybe you have drawn a box around God too. If you have decided that He works only in certain ways and not in ways unfamiliar to you, then you have a box. If you have rejected "fullness of the Holy Spirit" teaching in the past, I want to assure you that God is outside your box, waiting for you to peek around the walls of your knowledge and see Him as He is. Working powerfully in the lives of believers through the fullness of His Spirit.

As women in love with God, we have certain responsibilities that come with our relationship. Of primary importance is that you and I make our hearts available to God's desire to fill us with the Spirit. In this chapter, as much as I know how, I want to continue to direct you in this journey toward the fullness of the Spirit.

Years ago, someone asked me, "If the Holy Spirit were to leave you, would you even know that He was gone?" That question persists in my spirit and daily shapes my study and my prayers. I desire to walk with such intimacy and dependence that I can sense the indwelling of the Spirit. Know His voice. Wait for His fullness.

After the very deliberate decision to become more aware of the presence of the Spirit and to pursue His filling, there is our everyday, moment-to-moment walk with God. In recent years, I have begun every day with two prayer requests and then asked myself several ongoing questions during the day. I share these with you for the sake of discipleship. You do not have to make them yours, but I'm praying that you are prompted to formulate your own heart-check questions.

Two Requests

Every morning, before I am even out of bed, I ask God to refill me anew with the gift of His Spirit.

> *Father, would You come this morning and fill me afresh with the presence and power of the Holy Spirit?*

Charles Ryrie said:

> *The most distinguishing feature of filling is that it is a repeated experience . . . That it can be repeated is a blessing, for if it were not so, no believer would remain filled for long, since sin breaks the control of the Spirit.*[3]

Then I ask God to make me aware of any part of me that might quench or hinder the presence of the Spirit. First Thessalonians 5:19 says, "Do not hold back the work of the Holy Spirit" (NCV).

> *God, point out to me any sin or attitude that will keep the Holy Spirit from working in my life today.*

I am not without sin, but I can be made clean every day through prayer and God's forgiveness.

I was on a plane a few weeks ago and sat beside a guy who had several vodka tonics before we left the ground. Eventually, there was a conversation, and he told me he was on his way to propose to his girlfriend. A little later he said, "Yeah, almost every area of my life is really great right now, except me and God."

I smiled to myself. Divine appointment. I love it when God puts me where He wants me to speak His tender love into someone's life.

"So what's up with you and God?" I asked.

"I go to church and everything. It's just that I still struggle with the same old sins and sometimes I don't even care. Then when I don't care, I feel guilty. And when I feel guilty, then I stay away from God. Right now I'm away from God because I keep taking His name in vain. I hate myself for it. But I just won't seem to stop."

We had a great conversation for the next hour about the age-old frustration of repetitive sin and the timeless truth of God's forgiveness. Just as we were landing he asked me, "Do you think I'll ever really get past this same old stuff?"

I knew I could run down the aisle in just a minute and never see this man again, so from a tender confidence I said to him, "One day you'll decide that you've had enough of the childishness and realize it's time to grow up. You'll listen to the voice of the Holy Spirit speaking softly inside you and you'll respond to His promptings with obedience. Right now you're battling your immature faith. But that could all change as soon as you're ready."

I braced myself, waiting for the weight lifter in the window seat to turn away or look offended by my words. Instead, he looked at me as though he'd never thought of listening to the Holy Spirit before in his life. He told me thanks, and then as we stood waiting to exit the plane, he said, "You should keep talking to people about God." I told him I would.

It was so easy to relate to my seat buddy on the plane. I have been where he is. So many times I have wanted to kick myself across the room because I'm praying worn-out prayers asking God to forgive me of the same sin. Here is what we can come to terms with. We will continue to deal with sin. But by the power of the Holy Spirit, you and I can grow up and find big and small victories over besetting sins.

> *So, my brothers and sisters, we must not be ruled*
> *by our sinful selves or live the way our sinful selves*
> *want. If you use your lives to do the wrong things your*
> *sinful selves want, you will die spiritually. But if you*
> *use the Spirit's help to stop doing the wrong things you*
> *do with your body, you will have true life.*
>
> (Romans 8:12–13 NCV)

Ask God every day to point out to you what separates you from Him. He will give you discernment. Each day, you and I need new discernment. But you will know that you are beginning to grow up when discernment is all you need. With maturity comes the decision not to debate anymore. You no longer have to argue about whether or not you will accept the Spirit's prompting. When you have received the discernment, your heart is ready to obey.

There is still sin for me to repent of. But with maturity, many of my old blatant sins have lost their allure. And with even greater maturity, old habits that lead to sin are being defeated.

Ongoing Questions

My girlfriend said to me the other day, "I had forgotten that the Holy Spirit is the third part of the Trinity, equal in importance to

God the Father and God the Son, Jesus. He is God's presence on this earth in this age. He is God's hand to hold and God's voice to listen for. I have been spending weeks coming to understand His importance in my life."

How many of us probably feel the same way? We have forgotten about the weight and significance of the Holy Spirit. He is in and around us, and yet we miss the glory of His presence. But that is the work of Satan. His chief concern is that we do not see the glory of God. And very specifically, if you have not given much thought to the work and the magnitude of the Spirit in your life, then you are actively missing the glory.

Paul tells us about these designs of Satan in 2 Corinthians 4:4 (NCV):

> *The devil who rules this world* has blinded the minds of those who do not believe. *They cannot see the light of the Good News—the Good News about the glory of Christ, who is exactly like God.* (emphasis mine)

One of the ongoing questions that we can ask ourselves is: *Am I seeing the glory of God?*

When we can see the glory of God, then we want to honor the Christ of that glory. We want to see more of the Holy Spirit's efforts around us. We want to celebrate His goodness and worship His splendor.

Another question is: *Am I being led by the Holy Spirit?*

I find myself with this question most often when I am disciplining the children or searching for a way to unlock their hearts or give guidance. Many times I will be talking to a woman at a conference and I have to wait to respond to her until I believe I am being led by God's indwelling. Sometimes after a woman has told me her circumstances, I'll realize that I don't have any idea what to say to her. Several times I have asked if I can e-mail her later or speak to her at another break. I don't want to give her anything until I believe I am being led by the Spirit.

God has every answer that we need. He is always willing to lead in your decisions and your words. Romans 8:14 (NCV) puts it this way:

> The true children of God are those who let God's Spirit lead them.

And then Paul wrote in Galatians:

> Live by following the Spirit.
> (5:16 NCV)

> We get our new life from the Spirit, so we should follow the Spirit.
> (5:25 NCV)

You can know that you are being led by the Spirit in a few ways:

- Your actions or choices will not run counter to any teaching from Scripture.
- The Spirit makes your desire to please God stronger

than your desire to operate according to your flesh
or please only yourself.

- Being led by the Spirit brings freedom
  (2 Corinthians 3:17) instead of feeling you are
  forced to obey a law with one arm twisted behind
  your back. Obedience in the Spirit brings joy
  instead of a burden.
- The woman who is being led by the Spirit is a
  woman characterized by loving behavior
  (Galatians 5:13–14).
- Being led by the Spirit produces the fruit of the Spirit
  in your everyday, moment-by-moment life. Love,
  joy, peace, patience, kindness, goodness, faithfulness,
  gentleness, and self-control (Galatians 5:22–23).
- The heart being led by the Spirit is thankful for
  every enablement and gift that God brings. A
  woman full of the Spirit is truly grateful.

Every once in a while, one of the children will do the same old
thing, like throw their dirty clothes behind the door in the bathroom, and from somewhere I hadn't expected, I will hear myself
respond to them in a fresh, new way. My discipline to them comes
through words of patience and self-control. And I will know that I
am being led by the Spirit. When I was a young believer, acting in
obedience felt like a duty, but as I desire more to walk by the Spirit,
obedience is producing a freedom and a joy that I did not know in
those early years.

The next question that should work its way through our spiritual
lives is: *Am I praying in the Spirit?*

Several times in the Bible, we are directed to pray in the Spirit:

> *Pray in the Spirit at all times with all kinds of prayers, asking for everything you need. To do this you must always be ready and never give up.*
>
> (Ephesians 6:18 NCV)

> *Use your most holy faith to build yourselves up, praying in the Holy Spirit.*
>
> (Jude 20 NCV)

Praying in the Holy Spirit means that we are moved to pray and are guided in prayer by the Spirit. In the Ephesians passage above, Paul says that all our prayer is to be offered in the Spirit, so praying in the Spirit isn't just some different form of praying; it's how God expects we will learn to pray.

In Romans 8:26 (NCV), Paul wrote about praying in the Spirit:

> *Also, the Spirit helps us with our weakness. We do not know how to pray as we should. But the Spirit himself speaks to God for us, even begs God for us with deep feelings that words cannot explain.*

So we know that the Holy Spirit helps us in our weakness, even our weak praying.

Praying in the Spirit enables us to pray in ways we could not on our own. Perhaps the question rising inside you at this point is one that I have dealt with: *How do I know that I am praying in the Spirit?* As I realized that I could pray in my own strength or I could pray in the power of the Spirit, I truly desired the latter, but how? No one ever taught me to "pray in the Spirit." I have come to understand two very important elements that we can apply and then rest in.

First, to pray in the Spirit requires your faith. A determined faith in the promises of Jesus. He sent the Spirit to all believers, including you and me, and we can fully rest the weight of our prayers on that promise. I have said to God something like this:

> *God, I want to pray in the power of the Holy Spirit.*
> *All I can give You are my desires. I want to honor You*
> *in my words and my emotions. I want to surrender my*
> *thoughts to You. I realize that I cannot pray as I should*
> *without the Spirit, so I make Him welcome in my life,*
> *and I trust Him to perfect my prayers.*

And second, to pray in the Spirit requires that we pray according to God's Word. Second Peter 1:21 (NCV) says:

> *No prophecy ever came from what a person wanted*
> *to say, but people led by the Holy Spirit spoke words*
> *from God.*

I am learning in my daily Bible reading to not only think about how to apply a certain passage to my life, but how to pray that passage for my family and myself.

While we are talking about praying in the Spirit, it's very important that we consider "listening" to the Holy Spirit. If your life is anything like mine, finding time to pray or stop for a few minutes to read the Bible is a big deal. So, stopping to "listen" to the Holy

Spirit hasn't been on the radar very much. But I don't think we can proceed or expect to grow in our faith without a sincere understanding of how important it is to "listen" for the Spirit of God.

With all the voices in my head and the lists I'm always making, I hear a lot going on, but I have decided that I want to know the voice of the Holy Spirit above all that. I want to recognize His voice the way I can hear a cough in the next room and tell you which one of my children it belongs to. For a very long time, I assumed that the Holy Spirit would be louder. That He would yell through the chaos and shout His orders to me. I am learning that the Holy Spirit is tender. His promptings are gentle and His voice is soft, spoken in a deep place inside me.

If He is soft and gentle, then I have to stop, really stop my mind and my surroundings to listen. I want to hear from the Holy Spirit all during the day, but most assuredly before I begin my day. If I wake up before my alarm, before anyone else is stirring, I lie there and ask God to let me hear the Spirit's voice. As I get up, I move through the house in quiet, trying to listen for the gentle One before the craziness starts.

The Holy Spirit's voice is not an obsessive voice you hear over and over in your mind. His is not the accusing speech or the discouraging tone that feeds your depression. His words are not pessimistic, and they do not cause you to fall into despair.

The Holy Spirit speaks what He hears from the Father. He speaks of your certain hope. He guides you into greater faith. He gives a holy comfort from the One who is eternally in love with you. He guides you into wisdom. He teaches you to dance in the arms of the Father.

Listening to the Spirit will require an effort on your part. But the act of listening will bring peace to your chaos. The listening will cause you to stop and ask the One who is waiting to respond. Choosing to listen will strengthen your faith. When you learn to hear from the Holy Spirit and then react according to His guidance, there is a peaceful, righteous confidence that will cause you to trust even more the faithfulness of God.

You Are Important and Precious and Beautiful

When I am at home with the kids, fairly sure of my surroundings and my value, I walk around in old jeans, pull my unstyled hair into a ponytail, and go without makeup for days. At home I can be myself. I am accepted. Loved. Enjoyed. Piddling around in my own kitchen, I am without many of the insecurities that can come to us in unfamiliar surroundings. Maybe one of the most vital characteristics of a healthy relationship or a healthy family is the presence of complete acceptance. That's what love does. It loves entirely, without condition and without hesitation.

That same complete acceptance should mark our relationship with God. But more often than not, many of us have come to believe God's love for us is reluctant, something He gives only in response to requirements met and services rendered. Sometimes when you have not known healthy love, it's difficult to envision a heavenly Father whose love is so pure. Here is where I believe the Holy Spirit can move us into a greater confidence regarding the love of God. Listen to these words of truth for you in Romans:

> *The Spirit we received does not make us slaves again to fear; it makes us children of God. With that*

Spirit we cry out, "Father." And the Spirit himself
joins with our spirits to say we are God's children.

(8:15–16 NCV)

You are a child of God. Really and truly. In the family.
Important. Precious. Beautiful. There is enough healthy love to go
around. There is an even more complete acceptance. It's a truth you
can build your whole life on. But maybe your heart hesitates. Maybe
you are afraid that something doesn't make this completely true for
you. Go back and read the first line of this passage. The Spirit takes
away those fears. The Spirit is sure that you are a daughter of your
heavenly Father. It's all been settled. God's love for you is unceasing
and extravagant.

Ask God to convince you of this truth through the work of His
Spirit. To persuade you that nothing, absolutely nothing, can separate you from His love. That He is your companion and friend for all
eternity. That His love for you is not wishy-washy or undecided.
There is a God in heaven who is absolutely in love with you, and by
the testimony of the Holy Spirit, you can live and dance in that truth.
It is the work of the Holy Spirit to give you an unshakable confidence
in God's love for you. He is able to replace your doubts with certainty. You belong to God. He calls you His. His love never fails.

Worship in the Spirit

Every time I teach the truth of God's unending work in our
lives, His deep love that never gives up on me, His ongoing forgiveness, His new mercy and fresh start every single morning—
then I remember anew why we worship.

Who, me? You're calling my name when no one else will? No one else sees. No one comes to me except You.

Eyes full of tears over Your mercy.

For me? You'd wipe the slate clean for me? You promise to forget my sins again? There is no one else like You.

Incomprehensible mercy. My heart fills with gratitude.

You ask me to come closer. Draw near to You. Let Your strength embrace me. Feel Your tenderness heal me.

What kind of love is this?

You want me to look into Your eyes. Trust You. Dance with You.

Teach me how to worship this God of love with my life.

The Scriptures very specifically teach us to worship in the Spirit:

> *God is spirit, and those who worship him must worship in spirit and truth.*
>
> (John 4:24 NCV)

> *We worship God through his Spirit.*
>
> (Philippians 3:3 NCV)

I believe that when we have made a commitment to seek the filling and the power of the Holy Spirit, this worship is the overflow of gratitude that wells up within us. It's why we shout "Hallelujah!" It's the reason we lift our hands in surrender to our great and merciful God. We sing and pray and bow in reverence. Heartfelt praise and worship are the marks of a real experience of the Holy Spirit. When the Spirit directs our worship, the heart filled with gratefulness then does the only thing we know to do as humans—we live and breathe an offering of praise for our Creator.

Paul says it perfectly in Romans 12:

> *So brothers and sisters, since God has shown us great mercy, I beg you to offer your lives as a living sacrifice to him. Your offering must be only for God and pleasing to him, which is the spiritual way for you to worship.*
>
> (v. 1 NCV)

What wondrous love is this, O my soul, O my soul. Charles Ryrie said this about our growth:

> *Maturity involves two things—time and continued control by the Holy Spirit. Thus a person may be immature either because [she] has not been a Christian very long or because, even though [she] has been a believer for a time, [she] has not been filled by the Spirit and therefore has not had any growth in the things of the Lord.*[4]

So that you and I will become the women God intended— mature, confident, dancing in the light of His love—this teaching about the Holy Spirit is required application. Spiritual wallflowers stay that way apart from the filling and power of the Holy Spirit.

a dancing lesson

The wallflower, who never
thought it possible, can be
filled to the measure of all
fullness by the amazing
presence and power of
the Holy Spirit. That
fullness brings a
righteous confidence, and
that's when wallflowers begin to dance.

KNOWLEDGE OF THE Father's heart is usually not given to a casual inquirer. It is mostly given to the diligent seeker.

—*Mark Pate*

MATURITY IS NOT a spiritual gift nor is it a by-product of salvation. It is something we as Christians must work on our entire lives.[1]

chapter nine

No Matter What

Last week, my children and I drove to North Carolina to visit my aging grandmother, Ima. She is eighty-nine and has had several small strokes in the past few years. Her mind isn't very clear about today or yesterday, but she still remembers the minute details of decades ago, especially if the story is funny—and when she's doing the telling, everything is funny to Ma-Ma.

Geneva stays with my grandmother during the day, and a woman named Hattie—almost the same age as my grandmother—comes to take care of her every night. It had been too long since all the children had been for a visit; some of them couldn't remember their great-grandmother very well. They weren't sure what to expect, and I wasn't really sure how our time would go. I just knew we needed to go. I thought that she needed to see us all together. Turns out, it was the five of us who needed to see her.

The night we got there, Ma-Ma was sitting in her La-Z-Boy watching the *Wheel of Fortune*. Hattie sat beside her in a glider rocker. And most of the evening these women in their late eighties held hands. Ma-Ma was dressed in navy blue dress pants with a smart argyle sweater vest. She'd been to the beauty shop a few days before. I thought she looked wonderful. But what made her beautiful was her smile.

Ma-Ma lit up when all the children came in. Hugs for everybody. Laughter. Little kisses of delight. And lots of stories. Just the same as she's always been from my very first memories of her. Always laughing and dancing. Always, always finding what's good, what's lovely, and what's hopeful.

That night the stories began with the day of my dad's birth. He weighed ten pounds and four ounces. "Yep, yer PaPa's always been big." And wound up with the one about her new lower bed that keeps her from falling in and out. "These days when I fall, I just stay down there." She laughed, then deadpanned to Hattie, "I won't get that drunk next time."

The children were mesmerized. Most of them hadn't been old enough to enjoy how entertaining their great-grandmother has always been, and that night they focused intently on everything she said and did. She made my really cool fifth-grade son repeatedly laugh out loud, which gives her highest comedic honors in my book. I dare anybody else to make that happen.

As soon as we got outside that night, all the kids were talking a mile a minute.

"Mom, Great-grandma is really funny."

"Of course she is. Where do you think you get it from?"

"She was kidding about the getting drunk part, right?"

"Yep, just kidding."

Our visit to my grandmother's house was one of the best trips we've ever taken. Those two days were a powerful affirmation of everything I have been taught and observed all my life. During that visit, I realized Ma-Ma is finishing well. Her physical and mental capacities are diminished, but her spirit is strong. Her soul is fully at peace. Her confidence is righteous. Her life has been well lived.

When I lay the life I desire to live beside the gracious life my grandmother has already lived, I realize there are some core values and characteristics that you and I must practice and hold on to, no matter what. I realize it's a battle to hang on through the most difficult of circumstances, but I have witnessed the fruit of these characteristics lived, and here is what we have to do, no matter what.

Believe God, No Matter What

This very morning, the headline on my Internet news page reads, "Famous Atheist Now Believes in God." Read for yourself:

> NEW YORK Dec 9, 2004—A British philosophy professor who has been a leading champion of atheism for more than a half-century has changed his mind. He now believes in God more or less based on scientific evidence, and says so on a video released Thursday.
>
> At age 81, after decades of insisting belief is a mistake, Antony Flew has concluded that some sort of intelligence or first cause must have created the universe. "A super-intelligence is the only good explanation for the origin of life and the complexity of nature," Flew said in a telephone interview from England.[2]

Flew said, "My whole life has been guided by the principle of Plato's Socrates: Follow the evidence, wherever it leads."

After a lifetime of study and ardent unbelief, the "evidence" has led a world-renowned atheist to believe in a Creator God.

I know that sometimes you can't see God or feel God or understand God. First Corinthians 13:12 NKJV says that in this life *we see in a mirror, dimly*. But your lack of seeing or feeling or understanding does not make the reality of God any less. The truth of His existence is not diminished by doubts or distractions. Listen to God speaking:

> The LORD says, *"You are my witnesses and the servant I chose.*
>
> *I chose you so you would know and believe me, so you would understand that I am the true God.*
>
> *There was no God before me, and there will be no God after me.*
>
> *I myself am the LORD;*
>
> *I am the only Savior.*
>
> *I myself have spoken to you, saved you, and told you these things.*
>
> *It was not some foreign god among you.*
>
> *You are my witnesses, and I am God,"* says the LORD.
>
> *"I have always been God."*
>
> (Isaiah 43:10–13 NCV)

No matter what comes to you or what never does, one truth still holds: Our God is alive. He is real. Trust your life to Him. Believe Him more than anything. Will you believe now through anything or will you wait like the atheist for eighty-one years to bow your life before Him?

Live with Integrity, No Matter What

Most of the women I meet are not struggling with big, fat, in-your-face sin. They're too smart and the consequences are too devastating. It's the little stuff in the unseen that stacks up and becomes consuming. Then one day, the woman who never saw it coming is in a counselor's office, saying, "I don't know how this happened." Little choices. Tiny lies. So many regrets.

You've heard it since grade school: integrity is what you do when no one's looking. And integrity no matter what will set your life apart. God sees and He smiles, then He blesses.

Maybe you know other Christians who seem to "get away" with so much more than your conscience will allow. You watch their private choosing and scratch your head. *Why can't I live like that or choose like that or cheat like that?* Keep watching. Our God will not be mocked.

You have to do the right thing, no matter what. Even if it's not to your advantage, or could cost you money or reputation, you have to walk with integrity. If you are unsure what to do next, then just keep doing the last thing you know for sure that came from God. Stay with it, honestly and with integrity. The rewards for choosing rightly, no matter what, may take part of a lifetime to come to you, but I promise that God will honor your private strength, and until then, your integrity will keep you sleeping like a baby.

Stay in a Bible-Believing Church, No Matter What

Even though I am committed to getting there, some days I just don't feel like going to church. My flight got in late the night before,

I drove from the airport in the rain, hauled my bags upstairs, looked through the mail, and then took another hour to fall asleep around 2:00 a.m. Besides, I am usually in a church somewhere all weekend with a lot of worship music and praying and ministry going on.

It doesn't matter. Being in somebody else's church all weekend doesn't mean I've been to my church. My body. Heard from my Shepherd. Looked into the eyes of my accountability. Sometimes I'm all talked out, and the last thing I want to do is go where a group of people might want to talk. Doesn't really matter. This one's not about me. It's about God. He has promised to use His church. He shows up there.

I happen to go to a great church where everyone is in process. We love God and we fail sometimes and we try to figure it out and get back in there. Lately I've talked to several Christians who haven't been to church in a couple of years. They got mad about something or they got their feelings hurt or they have some bona fide reason not to ever go back to that place again. I get it. Sometimes you land in the wrong place and you need to get to the right place. But no matter what, you can't stop showing up somewhere, especially not for years.

Just in case you're wondering, a Bible study with your girlfriends is not a substitute for church. It's a good thing, but not a church. No matter where it meets—a building, a home, or temporarily in a theater—a church has a pastor, elders and/or deacons, and a bunch of other sinners who come to hear from God.

Keep Reading the Bible, No Matter What

Jesus says to us in John 15:7 (NIV):

If you remain in me and my words remain in you,
ask whatever you wish, and it will be given you.

I realize that you already have heard and believe in the importance of reading the Bible. It's just that very few of us have made a commitment to stay in the words of God, no matter what. Even when your heart is dry. Even when you feel no emotion or seem to get nowhere with the passage. Stay in there and keep these anointed words "abiding" in your mind and heart. Remember these reasons to study the Bible from the book of Psalms:

The teachings of the LORD are perfect; they give new strength.
The rules of the LORD can be trusted; they make plain people wise.
The orders of the LORD are right; they make people happy.
The commands of the LORD are pure; they light up the way.

(19:7–8 NCV, emphasis mine)

Plan how you are going to read the Bible so that you don't get it in your hand and have no idea where to turn. Keep a Bible in every room of your house and in the car so that it's always within reach. Read different versions of Scripture to hear a fresh understanding of a passage you've heard only a certain way. Memorize the books of the Bible in order so that it's easy to get around and you feel comfortable finding your way.

This year I'm reading through the New Century Version of the

Bible. That time of reading, underlining, and praying is all for me. It's not a time to study for writing or teaching. It's the time I want to hear from God for my daily life and my family.

As you make this commitment to consistently read the Bible, everything in the world will happen to distract you from keeping it. Realize what's happening. A spiritual battle. Stay in there. Fight to get to the Word. God has promised that His words will never return void. That means His words will always be powerful, especially when they have been taken deep into your life. Daily, no matter what, keep reading and meditating on God's words to you.

Keep Praying, No Matter What

Henri Nouwen wrote:

> *I am called to enter into the inner sanctuary of my own being where God has chosen to dwell. The only way to that place is prayer, unceasing prayer. Many struggles and much pain can clear the way, but I am certain that only unceasing prayer can let me enter it.* [3]

Every time I think that I don't really feel like praying, a spiritual siren goes off in my head. It's loud and obnoxious and it's screaming, *Then you really need to pray!* We've already covered so much about the how-to's of prayer. But as a reflection of your spiritual character, it has to be a no matter what.

When It's Dark, Don't Move, No Matter What

God always comes. If you find yourself in an emotional or spiritual darkness or without any sense of God's direction, then don't move. Wait on God. Trust His promises to you. Sit still. Don't take one step until God comes to show you the way.

I wish with all my heart I could tell you that every day for me is a day in the light of Jesus. I have read some of the words of other believers, and it seems they eventually get there in their spiritual maturity. I honestly struggle with days of deep darkness and clouds. On those days, I still believe God. I know Him to be true more than I know anything. I imagine that there is a brightness somewhere, but I know only dark, and I struggle with waves of depression. My loneliness is almost overwhelming. I want to give up. Cry until I'm empty. Anything to get away from the darkness.

I can write these words on this day, because God is just bringing me into the dawn, again. You know one day of soul midnight is not so bad, but when it becomes five or ten days in a row, the heart grows exhausted and weary. The past few days, my kids would ask, "Mom, what's wrong?" "I think I'm just tired" was all I could give them. I have been tired, but not physically—just tired of the dark. And when it's this dark, no one else can understand how you got there or why their well-intended words can't get you out.

As a woman, the first thing I jump to when emotional clouds roll in is PMS. But when my darkness doesn't coincide with PMS, I know something is really wrong. This past week wasn't PMS. Just thick and black and suffocating. I knew it was a spiritual battle. So, I asked people to pray for me. I got up every day and did what I knew to do, no matter what. Nothing happened. No big surge of emotional energy. No spiritual breakthroughs. No phone calls to make everything all better. But I've been through this before and I knew not to move. Just sit in the dark without taking a step until Jesus comes.

Last night around seven, I felt the bondage of darkness begin to break. Absolutely nothing special had happened in my physical world to make things better. Yesterday was just about like the five before it. Kids, house, errands, e-mails, work. But before I went to bed, I knew that the clouds of my heart were stirring. I prayed again before I went to sleep and begged God to come and fill me afresh with His Spirit. I've prayed that way every day, but this morning God came. Today I can see again. Spiritual eyes have returned. My spiritual energy renewed. Finally, I have a clarity and a confidence I haven't known for days.

So what is this darkness that comes to us? Sometimes it is the consequence of our own choosing. We've become lazy or distant from God and so we can't see Him. Sometimes it's the result of continuing in sin or destructive behavior. But what about when those don't seem to be the case? You've been pursuing God. You've asked Him to reveal any sin or any hindrance that would keep you in the dark. You've asked for forgiveness and best as you know, you are clean and persevering in the faith. Then what?

Then I believe we're in a spiritual battle. One being fought in the heavenlies on our behalf. And we shouldn't move in any direction until God shows up. Do you remember the story in Daniel? Daniel had been praying and waiting on God. An angel showed up in chapter 10 and said:

Daniel, do not be afraid. Some time ago you decided to get understanding and to humble yourself before your God. Since that time God has listened to you, and I have come because of your prayers. But the prince of Persia has been fighting against me for twenty-one days. Then Michael, one of the most important angels, came to help me, because I had been left there with the king of Persia. Now I have come to explain to you what will happen to your people.

(Daniel 10:12–14 NCV)

The angel coming to Daniel was delayed twenty-one days because on the way there was a fight with Satan. Such an intense fight that the archangel Michael had to come and help. I am not a spiritual battle scholar, but I do know this: God fights for us in the unseen. We don't know why it takes so long sometimes, but we can trust His faithfulness.

Yesterday I told my girlfriend, "I hate this darkness, but as far as I know, I am clean and I believe that God is coming. All I know to do is just get up again tomorrow and trust Him still. I have learned the hard way, don't do anything until the way is clear. Do not make a personal or family decision in the dark."

I have waited to sign new contracts until I believed I was going forward in the light of understanding and God's guidance. I don't accept speaking engagements if there seems to be darkness blocking my sight or my decision. I wait to give the children permission for trips or other decisions until I believe we are proceeding in the light.

In the dark, don't quit what you're doing or commit to anything new. If you have doubts, then don't. Until God takes hold of your hand to lead you out, then no matter how dark, don't move.

Laugh Every Time You Can, No Matter What

As we sat in the living room with my grandmother, watching her laugh and make us laugh, I knew that her infectious lightheartedness had served her and our family well. She taught us all to laugh, sometimes at ourselves but mostly by finding humor in the circumstances. Rich or poor, through health and celebration or death and grieving.

She taught us all how to tell a good story and wait just the right length of time to spring the punch line. She gave each one of us the tool of harmless exaggeration that keeps us all trying to get a bigger laugh. She taught us that taking yourself too seriously makes you look ridiculous. My grandmother has lived her whole life just as God meant for us to laugh. I believe she is right.

You have to wake up and observe life to find what's funny or amusing. You have to be a student of wisdom in order to realize when something is witty. I believe that you can learn to laugh. I believe that God gives a cheerful disposition and a light heart when we give Him the heavy yoke of our burdens.

A lifetime of laughter and dancing. I think it should be a required character trait of the godly woman, no matter what.

Enjoy God's Good Gifts, No Matter What

A father gives his daughter a gift. A good and thoughtful gift that he has chosen just for her. A gift that he knew she desired and longed for. The loving father waited until just the right moment and then he gave his special gift, beautifully wrapped, anticipating his daughter's delight. Then the father watched as his child unwrapped the gift, looked at its contents, and then laid it aside without emotion or thankfulness. The father's heart was broken. He wanted to bless his daughter, but she had not enjoyed his good gift to her.

Our heavenly Father gives good gifts to those He loves. Look around you this very moment and see with your eyes, feel with your heart, all His goodness for you. He meant for you to enjoy each of His gifts. Delight in their goodness. Celebrate His love for you. Share what you have been given.

The book of Ecclesiastes echoes this refrain over and over through its chapters: "Love God and enjoy your life." Time goes by, meaningless pursuits distract us, but no matter what, love Him and enjoy the goodness of His gifts.

Love Your Family Well, No Matter What

I don't mean to, but sometimes I miss my book deadlines. It frustrates a lot of people, but in a pinch, and there seem to be a lot of them in this family, I always have to go with what matters most. A single mom with four kids and a full-time career don't really go together. No one could get all this done. I do the best I can and then when there's a conflict or a standoff, I am deciding to always choose love. Watch AnnaGrace be the lazy brown bear in her first-grade play right in the middle of the day or finish another thousand words. It's not even an issue anymore. Love wins.

This year the kids and I bought a house. A really great house that had been cared for. The family before us left it almost perfect. No weeds in the yard, no worn-out grass under the swing. I wanted to keep it just the way we found it. My dad took me out on the deck the day we were moving in and said, "After the kids are gone, you'll have plenty of time to grow grass, the carpets will be spotless, and there won't be any scooters junking up the garage. That day is coming much too soon." I got it. After the kids are gone, I'll probably turn my books in early too.

In the end, our accomplishments will be forgotten. The lawn will be manicured. The laundry room will be empty. The books will go out of print and eventually be sold for a dollar at the discount warehouse. Someone else will come along who can say it better and funnier. So right now, when push comes to shove and something's gotta give, love your family, no matter what.

When it was time to leave my grandmother, I leaned in for one last hug. She pulled me close with more strength than I anticipated and held me longer than I had expected. Then she said to me, "Angela, I love you a bushel and a peck and a hug around the neck. But you already know that."

I couldn't breathe. Tears rushed to my eyes and begged to get out. I did know that. Of all the things I know for sure, my family's love is certain. She has spoken those words to me all of my life, but in that instant I felt the enormity of being covered with consistent, lavish love. The gift of being loved first, no matter what. It took all my air away. Still does.

What do I want my family to know for sure, no matter what? Underneath their belief in God, what one thing will give them security and strength and confidence?

What will teach them goodness and structure their priorities as adults? *If they know I love them a bushel and a peck and a hug around the neck. And every day we live it, no matter what.*

a dancing lesson

Beginning to dance is
showing up where God is,
no matter what, believing
in the power of His
unfailing love, no matter
what, and persevering through
each lesson—no matter what.

WE TALK AS IF it were the most precarious thing to live the sanctified life; it is the most secure thing, because it has Almighty God in and behind it.[1]

GOD DID NOT give us a spirit that makes us afraid but a spirit of power and love.

—*2 Timothy 1:7 NCV*

THERE HAS NEVER been the slightest doubt in my mind that the God who started this great work in you would keep at it and bring it to a flourishing finish on the very day Christ Jesus appears.

—*Philippians 1:6 THE MESSAGE*

FINALLY, BE STRONG in the Lord and in his great power.

—*Ephesians 6:10 NCV*

chapter ten

Becoming Brave... and Dancing

My baby girl ran to me after church while I was standing outside visiting with my girlfriends. I took AnnaGrace into my arms without thinking and without missing a beat in my grown-up conversation. After all these years, it's a pretty normal thing to have a kid hanging on to me somewhere, somehow. My youngest wrapped her arms around me and buried her head in my coat. I kept talking. She kept hugging.

After a while I realized that AnnaGrace was peeking out from my embrace and across the courtyard at her brothers. In a few minutes her peeking became more confident and eventually, my precious fourth-born was smiling like a beauty queen, dancing the happy dance and sticking out her tongue. My arms had become her refuge, and she was obnoxiously proud to be safe from the mean-boy taunting. The security of Mom even made her brave enough to yell, "Nah, nah, nah, you can't get me now."

AnnaGrace just turned seven. I'm her much older and wiser mom who longs for the same strong arms of protection and safety.

Almost all of my life I have been afraid. Afraid of failing. Afraid of success. Afraid of poverty. Afraid of wealth. Afraid of being alone. Afraid of too many people. I am such a weird contradiction of fears and insecurity. Whenever I was unsure, I instinctively held to the wallflower philosophy: "Don't let 'em see you at all." Disappear. Don't call attention to yourself. Lower your eyes and pray to evaporate.

When I was a little girl, all the neighborhood kids would play hide-and-go-seek in the houses under construction on our street. I can still remember hiding behind a piece of plywood and hearing the seekers walk past. I would hold my breath and try not to do anything that would reveal my presence and get me caught. Safety was knowing they'd gone to another location and they never even knew I was there.

When I have been afraid in life, I have played that same game in my head. *Where can I hide until this is over? Where can I go so that no one will know I'm not brave?* Sometimes we're mad that we've lived like a wallflower and other times, from fear, it's been our own choosing.

Maybe you have felt like a wallflower ever since the first day your kindergarten class went outside for recess. Maybe you've been noticed and then rejected and so you decided slipping into wallflower would spare you further pain. Maybe you've felt like a wallflower in your career or in your marriage or in friendship. Present but ignored. Seen but unknown.

I want to tell you something. Our Father sees you, and He sees me. You are not just a careless glance to Him. *The King is enthralled with your beauty.* Really. Truly.

He has great, big arms. They are strong and able to protect you. He expects that you would run to Him. Hide yourself in Him.

Find your refuge in Him. He promises to be your security and your defense. Just as AnnaGrace ran and hid herself in my love, we can run with our whole lives into the arms of God.

The wallflower stands alone in the shadows. Giving up. Going away. Becoming more and more the un-woman every day. The grown-up Jesus girl stands inside the arms of God, looking out at the great, big life still ahead. Safe. Secure. Dancing. Becoming brave.

When God walks into the room, wallflowers get to dance. Women who have been afraid become brave in His arms. Sure of His love, convinced of His faithfulness, a woman like you or me, one who has struggled with fear or insecurity or doubt, a woman like that can become a woman of righteous confidence.

Just in case it's been a while since you danced, may I remind you how it goes?

The Invitation

Because of His great love (*I have loved you with an everlasting love; I have drawn you with loving-kindness* [Jeremiah 31:3 NIV]), God invites you and me out of the shadows and into His arms. In Isaiah 55, God invites us to come to Him. There are two kinds of people who get invited. The first invitation is for the thirsty and the weak:

> *The LORD says, "All you who are thirsty, come and drink. Those of you who do not have money, come, buy and eat! Come buy wine and milk without money and without cost."*
>
> (Isaiah 55:1 NCV)

Maybe your heart is dry and parched. Maybe it hasn't rained in your soul for a very long time. Your hopes dried up years ago. Each path has been a dead end. Dreams are gone. Your life is numb. You never wanted to, but just to survive, you've become the un-woman who lives most every day just getting by. Then this invitation is for you.

But maybe that's not exactly where you are. But God calls another kind of woman in the next verse:

> *Why spend your money on something that is not*
> *real food? Why work for something that doesn't really*
> *satisfy you? Listen closely to me, and you will eat what*
> *is good; your soul will enjoy the rich food that satisfies.*
>
> (Isaiah 55:2 NCV)

He also calls the woman who is working and trying to live in strength but getting nowhere. She is not satisfied, but frustrated. This woman is still spending, still dreaming, still spinning the options. A different job. A new city. Another husband. But the new quickly fades, and the water she finds never seems to satisfy her thirst. Maybe that woman is you. Maybe you haven't given up, but you couldn't say that you live in the fullness of God's joy and dancing.

And so there are two kinds of people called. The thirsty who know they are bankrupt and cannot buy what they need. And the thirsty who have tried so hard to buy satisfaction that never comes. In the different seasons of my life, I have been both of those women. God tells us in verse 3 (NCV) to listen to His invitation:

> *Come to me and listen; listen to me so you may live.*

Listen this day. God is calling your name. Do you feel there has to be more? You thirst but cannot find water? You work but cannot be satisfied? Then God is calling you. Calling you alive by the power of His promises. Calling you into the life you were made for. Calling you from wallflower into a woman of righteous confidence.

According to Scripture, we are called and invited by God.

> *You are a chosen people, royal priests, a holy nation,*
> *a people for God's own possession. You were chosen to*
> *tell about the wonderful acts of God, who called you*
> *out of darkness into his wonderful light.*
>
> (1 Peter 2:9 NCV)

> *Those he planned to be like his Son, he also called;*
> *and those he called, he also made right with him; and*
> *those he made right, he also glorified.*
>
> (Romans 8:30 NCV)

Since the day you were born, God has been passionately in love with you, inviting you to dance the dance of your life in His arms. God does not call you from nothing into nothing. His invitation calls you to life. Enter into His promises and dance.

Your Response

God says to the wallflower, "May I have this dance?" Then He stands and waits. He waits for your delight. He waits for you to desire Him more than anyone or anything. He waits for your simple, "I'd love to." That same Isaiah passage continues:

> So you should look for the LORD before it is too late;
> you should call to him while he is near.
>
> (Isaiah 55:6 NCV)

Respond to God's invitation with your life. Run into the arms of God. Let His strength embrace you. Let His love hold you close.

Dancing

Almost every weekend I'm in a new place with new women. I never have any idea what to expect or what's coming this time. But I have learned not to be afraid, because I have become very confident that wherever I go, I go inside the arms of God. I am carried by His love. His protection surrounds me and defends me. He divinely orders my steps and ordains every encounter.

Sometimes I see myself inside God's arms like AnnaGrace getting away from her brothers. Even while He's busy running the whole wide world, He holds me inside His love and I am safe there. I peek out from those powerful arms and proudly mouth to anyone who sees, "I'm with Him."

Sometimes there can be very difficult circumstances and I will hear myself thinking to a person, *I don't think you understand whom I belong to. He's not going to allow this. Nobody treats His baby this way.*

Then I get so confident and secure right there with God that I picture me dancing. Definitely not the wallflower anymore. Dancing girl. Singing old Lionel Richie songs and doing the hustle.

Let's continue in this Isaiah passage and watch what happens from inside the arms of God.

> *So you will go out with joy and be led out in peace.*
> *The mountains and hills will burst into song before*
> *you, and all the trees in the fields will clap their hands.*
>
> (55:12 NCV)

When you and I are in the presence of God, there is joy. Singing. Clapping. Dancing. I don't think I'm stretching the passage too much. It sounds like the perfect place for dancing to me.

There is a truth that many of us miss. Somehow the world has convinced us that dancing happens apart from God. Somewhere out there, away from Him, we'll find ourselves. Become somebody. Find our passion. Find our place in this world. Then we'll dance.

But we were made for God. Created to live in His presence. Made to desire the water He offers for our thirst. When I spend time with the homeless women at missions around the country, they understand this next truth so well. Apart from God, as many of their lives testify, there is only bondage.

But when God takes us in His arms and draws us close to Him. When we begin to go where He leads, turn where He directs. Follow His steps. Grow in His love. When we are held so tightly in His divine strength that we hear His voice and move at His will, then we are finally free. Free and safe and dancing.

Free to Become

I have friends who think they're supposed to stay little in order to please God. Never have anything. Don't get too smart for your own good. Don't celebrate too loudly or too often. Don't make too much money. Remain hesitant and fearful out of some twisted version of reverence. Just calm it down for Jesus. Become enough, but not too much. You could get prideful. People might judge you wrongly. You'd struggle with selfish ambition.

But Scripture teaches us that we are free to become everything we can be for the glory of God on this earth. No holding back. No limits when it comes to the kingdom of heaven on earth. You're free to make your body and mind and spirit into the best, most lavish offering to God you can give.

Remember Jesus' story about this very idea in the parable of the talents?

> *A man going on a journey . . . called his servants and entrusted his property to them. To one he gave five talents of money, to another two talents, and to another one talent, each according to his ability. Then he went on his journey. The man who had received the five talents went at once and put his money to work and gained five more. So also, the one with the two talents gained two more. But the man who had received the one talent went off, dug a hole in the ground and hid his master's money.*
>
> (Matthew 25:14–18 NIV)

When the man returned to settle the accounts with his servants, do you remember what he said to the two who had multiplied their talents?

Well done, good and faithful servant! You have been faithful with a few things; I will put you in charge of many things. Come and share your master's happiness!

(Matthew 25:23 NIV)

And do you remember his response to the one who had buried all that he had been given?

Take the talent from him and give it to the one who has the ten talents. For everyone who has will be given more, and he will have an abundance. Whoever does not have, even what he has will be taken from him.

(Matthew 25:28–29 NIV)

Can you hear the heart of your Father in these words?

I want you to become everything I intended you to be. Invest your energies and your mind and your heart into multiplying your life and your person for My kingdom. You are free to take everything I have given to you, all the resources I have put inside you, and make them double! Whatever you become because of My presence in you is for My glory. Go get 'em, for goodness' sake! You are free and you are safe. Become strong. Become wise. Become confident.

Whatever I can do to encourage you, I want to do that. Life is whipping by. Too many people go to heaven wishing. Don't do that. Take these discipleship steps seriously and come into the light. Begin to grow in the characteristics of your faith and watch what God does in your life. Things are gonna change, and I mean *really*.

- When your heart gets set free from bondage, you get another chance.
- When your life gets clean, there is a fresh start bigger than the first day of next year.
- When fear begins to fade, a confidence comes to you that the world cannot have and Satan cannot steal.
- When you finally grow up into godliness, the love that you have multiplies in you and through you to everyone who bumps up against you. Can you imagine what that will do in the context of your family? Your marriage? Your friendships?
- When you start becoming God's woman, then God starts breaking heaven loose all over your circumstances.

I speak with incredible confidence concerning God's faithfulness. He will bless every place you multiply the talents He has given to you.

Free to Hope

Most of the time when we say, "I hope so," we mean, *I'm not really certain how it's going to turn out, but I'd really like for that to happen.* By and large, when we are "hoping" in our daily lives, we are in fact wishing and praying, but not certain.

That's not the kind of hope the New Testament writers talked about. Peter wrote in 1 Peter 1:13 (NIV):

> *Set your hope fully on the grace to be given you*
> *when Jesus Christ is revealed.*

Peter was not saying, "Sure would be nice if it turned out like that." As a matter of fact, there is no uncertainty expressed or implied. Peter was writing that our hope in Jesus is definite and firm. So when he said "hope fully" he meant without reservation or fear. Jesus is coming with grace for His people. Bank on it. Hope is a full assurance that God is going to deliver on every promise He has made.

But there is more to this hope we have in Jesus. Look at what Peter said at the beginning of the chapter:

> *Praise be to the God and Father of our Lord Jesus*
> *Christ. In God's great mercy* he has caused us to be
> born again into a living hope, *because Jesus Christ*
> *rose from the dead.*
>
> (1 Peter 1:3 NCV, emphasis mine)

Living hope is a hope that has power. Living hope takes the wallflower by the hand and walks her out of the dark and onto the dance floor. Living hope changes the way you look and act and think. Living hope is the fullness of the Holy Spirit transforming your attitudes and your actions.

Living hope comes to you, from God, for His glory. So that your life will radiate His brilliance. His mercy. His love. Living hope is a certain confidence that God has the power to change the way we live. God can multiply even the tiniest seeds, planted deeply within our souls, nourish them, and bear fruit in us that we could not even dream possible.

I don't know where you have been hedging on your hope. Afraid to hope for healing. Or love. Or dare to hope for your dreams. But it's time to set your hope free. You can hope like a woman of righteous confidence.

We have hope for only one reason, because of the grace of God.

> *May our Lord Jesus Christ himself and God our Father encourage you and strengthen you in every good thing you do and say. God loved us, and through his grace he gave us a good hope and encouragement that continues forever.*
>
> (2 Thessalonians 2:16–17 NCV)

Hope has come to us by grace. We can rejoice in that and be free to live in the certainty of that good hope from God.

Looking Out from the Arms of God

God steps into the shadows and says to the wallflower, "May I have this dance?"

And the wallflower, who's always been afraid of dancing, works up every bit of her courage to reply, "I'd love to."

As soon as the words leave her heart, the God of the whole universe takes the woman He loves into His arms. Big arms. Strong arms. The place she's always longed to be. He wraps her with a love that's safe and secure.

A distant sound becomes a symphony of music that stirs her soul. And before she knows what's happening, the wallflower who thought she never could, begins to dance.

But she hesitates, remembering that she doesn't know any of the steps.

Immediately, she feels His gentle touch and understands, *He is leading; I just have to follow.*

She wonders if someone might be watching.

And many are, because a woman held by God is captivating.

The dance makes her feel beautiful.

The dance of her life with God is everything she had always dreamed it could be.

She is safe.

He is strong.

She has been noticed and chosen and loved.

The wallflower looks out from the arms of God and finally knows . . . this is how a woman becomes brave. Being held in the arms of God and dancing gives a grace and a peace and a righteous confidence.

My dear friend, more than anything, I hope you dance.

a dancing lesson

When the wallflower begins
to dance, then all heaven
is eager to pour out the
riches of God for her life.
Glorious passion.
Extravagant hope. And the
assurance of righteous
confidence.

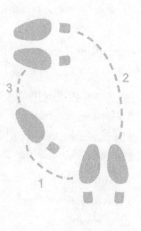

Those who danced
were thought to be quite insane
by those who could not
hear the music.

—Angela Monet

When You're Dancing

My friends Dave and Lisa brought their kids and came over for dinner a few nights ago. Dave told us about his day at work. The phones were out. The servers went down. Customers were extremely frustrated. He said the whole day was a disaster, and their company had never had a day like that. Lisa asked, "Did Angela drive by your office building today?" We all laughed.

The inside joke about my life is that wherever I am, things fall apart. You'd think that eventually enough things would come undone and then it would be over.

This morning I am writing in my study. I am bundled in several layers of clothes and a little space heater sits at my feet. It's January, and the downstairs furnace burned out about three weeks ago. The repair company finally received a new unit and made an appointment to do the install on Monday. But they called that morning and said all the repairmen have the flu and they'll get to us as soon as possible. That same afternoon, a neighbor knocked on my door to tell me the other heating unit, the one that was working upstairs, is completely frozen over, and he thinks I ought to turn it off. "Looks like it's low on Freon." Of course it is.

Two weeks ago, we were out of town and got the call that there was water gushing from our front yard. So much, in fact, that the whole street had turned to ice. We came home to burst pipes and no water for three days. Taking showers at the neighbors'. Going to the bathroom next door. Very inconvenient. Unfortunately, just another installment in our ongoing life saga.

I tell you all of this because I want you to hear these next words inside the context of my real life.

I am truly dancing in the arms of God.

My life is clean. My heart desires God more than anything. Every single day, I am doing the best I know how before the Lord. Caring for my children with compassion and love. Making decisions with the input of wise counsel. Seeking God's will. Surrendering my life. Worshiping. Believing. Waiting.

But dancing is not about finally getting to a perfect life without inconvenience or pain. I am dancing with God, but I have known some very deep, seemingly unwarranted, rejection. I am dancing, but pain has not been removed from my life. People disappoint us. Sickness surprises us. No one ever grows immune to the evil or the deceit among us. We live on this earth by God's grace and get to dance because of His presence and His filling. But life just keeps coming.

So if dancing isn't the easy life, then what in the world is it? Why should anybody want the spiritual maturity that becomes an intimate dance with God? What does it really matter about dancing if life is still hard and people hurt and things fall apart all around you?

Here is what it means to me to be dancing inside the strong arms of God.

Dancing Means That I Am Learning to Keep Eternity in View

Do you remember the book of Ecclesiastes? In that book, King Solomon is writing about what really matters. Maybe you remember that the first chapter of the book begins this way, " 'Meaningless! Meaningless!' says the Teacher. 'Utterly meaningless! Everything is meaningless' " (Ecclesiastes 1:2 NIV).

Solomon goes on to say wisdom is meaningless, pleasures are meaningless, work is meaningless, advancement is meaningless, riches are meaningless. And then there's the one verse that always gives perspective to my work: "Of making many books there is no end, and much study wearies the body" (Ecclesiastes 12:12 NIV). In effect, being a big-shot, best-selling author is meaningless.

Kind of depressing until you understand what Solomon wanted to say. Over and over in Ecclesiastes, he repeats, "Again I saw something meaningless *under the sun*" (4:7 NIV, emphasis mine). When you and I live *under the sun*, we see with earthly eyes, we feel with earthly disappointment, we groan with earthly pain. What is *above the sun* is eternal. Above the sun is what matters for God. And those pursuits are the only ones that give our lives true meaning.

Learning to live *above the sun* means that we are learning to keep eternity in view. When I am dancing in the arms of God, I hear Him whisper eternal truth, and it keeps my perspective clear. I feel in my spirit what matters to Him. And keeping eternity in mind takes the pressure off. Best-seller lists are cool, but what matters more is learning to hear the voice of my Father. Kids with straight A's are something to celebrate, but their grades are meaningless without tender hearts for God.

Dancing means that an eternal perspective keeps realigning your heart. Solomon says to "glorify God and enjoy His good gifts." When you keep that plain truth the main guiding truth, then you will step out of meaningless into all that matters. When you pull your life and your heart above the sun, with the God of eternity in view, then your everyday living becomes extraordinary dancing.

Dancing Means Persevering

I am not naturally ambitious or determined. No one who knows me would label me competitive or driven. A little discouragement used to send my heart packing. I would give up easily, surrender to defeat, and move on to something else. I wanted to persevere, but I was mostly a chicken.

Dancing means God has set me in motion and He is taking away my fears. Somehow, I just keep believing God and keep going no matter what. It's almost as if I am watching someone else persevere in spite of the obstacles, but it's just me, the old chicken being made into a woman who knows she is held and protected by her Father.

When you write and speak for a living, you can hear all kinds of things about yourself that make you want to quit. In a short amount of time I have heard:

Angela's too young for our event. Maybe she's too old. You are an amazing storyteller. Nope, you shouldn't tell so many stories; stay with the Bible teaching. Focus on your children, not your career. Career has to be first to take care of the children. We love your accent. Don't laugh like that. Don't bite your lip on camera. You're our favorite. Oops, now she's our favorite. Nice knowin' ya.

What people think and say can make you crazy. They misrepresent your heart and say things that make you want to throw up your hands and run. I realize that you don't have to write books to feel the conflict. I know that it happens in your circle of friends and at your work and in your family.

Here's the deal. You belong to God. You know where you are with Him, and that's all that matters. If God says you can, then keep going. If your life is clean, then keep going. If the Holy Spirit leads, then go. If you are dancing with God, people are gonna talk. They'll make you feel as if you shouldn't ever dance again.

Persevering means that you lean into God and proceed to dance around them.

∽

Dancing Means I Am Changing

God is opening my heart to new truth and new ways to live out that truth. In this next place with God, I have been made thirsty for greater spiritual depth, a desire for knowledge and its real-life application. I sense in my spirit that I am receptive to being changed and reshaped by God.

The old defiance of "I am who I am" has passed away; instead, when I pray to God, it sounds more like "Make me different. Make me Yours. Change me for Your glory."

Dancing Means I Am Smiling

Proverbs 31 says that a godly woman smiles at the future. I finally get it. We can smile because we know the heart of God. We trust because He has been more than faithful. We live surrendered and dependent because of His unfailing love. We exude confidence because He is in control. Sovereign. Guiding. All-powerful. Victorious.

Things fall apart and sometimes all hell breaks loose, but the woman who is dancing knows that God will break heaven loose over His Beloved. So she smiles, grateful to be held inside His love.

My friend, we are at the end of the book, and I am praying for you in these final words. I want you to get it. I want you to see *above the sun* of your situation. You do not have to live as the un-woman. Our circumstances will not be perfected until heaven, but you and I can dance here and now. And so, by the love of our Father, because of the resurrection of our Savior, Jesus, through the power of the Holy Spirit, do whatever it takes to grow up into His likeness, reorder your life around His love . . . and dance.

acknowledgments

I was at a neighbor's house a few weeks ago. Several families from our street were there to eat chili and watch a football game. During one of the commercials, we were lamenting the recent home disasters. My pipes breaking and making an ice rink at the bottom of the street, my pipes breaking again and forcing us to tote water in pails and use the bathroom next door for three days, my furnace burning up without a replacement for three cold weeks. Turns out that I won the home disaster contest that night, but at least they were good for a half-time laugh. Then one of the guys decides, "Maybe there should be a husband-on-call-beeper for you and we can all take turns wearing it." We all laughed about which poor guy would be on call for the next disaster of the week. But the truth is that everyone in my life is already on call, no beeper needed. I have all their numbers stored on speed dial.

First thing, I'd like to thank all the families in my neighborhood who take care of me and my children. The Striddes, Keyes, Sneeds, Dunns, Angels, Hahns, and Merritts. You bring in my trash can when I'm out of town, get the mail, hang pictures, help me crank the lawn mower, and drive my children to ball practice, guitar, and youth group. You invite us to dinner and bring us extra soup and cookies. I am so incredibly blessed to live beside you. God has given our family favor in giving us to you. My children are about to make me sign something notarized to promise that we'll never leave you.

Right there on my street is my friend Lisa Stridde. Lisa, I will never be able to say thank you enough. I am praying for God to reward you triple, because of your great friendship, love, and service to me, There is no way on this planet I could do anything I do without you. Your heart is so good. Your mind is so organized. Your commitment is steadfast. Thank you for making sure I make it, every single time.

Down the street, not far, is my friend Carla Martin. Carla, your friendship is such a treasure. Your heart for God inspires me. Thank you for the love and strength you have so freely given to me through all the years. Thank you for the powerful example of godliness you model with great consistency.

Only a mile away is the church I call home, safe haven, place of desperate worship, and classroom for my heart. Thank you to my pastors, elders, and gracious friends at Two Rivers Evangelical Free Church. Your covering is a gift from God and I know that.

I have to drive to Nashville to get to her, but my girlfriend Laura Johnson is worth it every mile. Laura, thanks for the sisterhood of our friendship. Thank you for the personal encouragement you have given to me over and over again. And to Christian, Simon, Holden, and Gillon, thanks for all the great life illustrations. I love you all. Let's go to the beach!

In Nashville is the team of folks who are always on call for me. My deepest thanks to Creative Trust Management, David, Dan, Jeanie, Jim, Lisa, Stephanie, Genesis, Amy, and Marianne. How in the world can I say thank you for believing and persisting and running ahead of me in everything I do? I love you and I promise to cook for you as often as possible to prove it. Jessica, your fingerprints are all over this project; thank you.

Also thanks to my brothers JT and Craig and their families for undying support and strength.

Across town is Thomas Nelson. Wow. Thank you for every opportunity you have given to me. Thank you for working so hard so that women all around the world can dance in the arms of God. Special thanks to Mike, Jonathan, Brian, Jerry, Kyle, and my new friend, Tami.

Also thanks to my friends at LifeWay, Dale, Lee, Betsy, Bill, Gena, and the whole print/video crew. What a great, great privilege to do incredible work alongside you.

Much too far away are some of my best friends in the world. Thank you, Dace, for every single theological discussion we have ever had. I believe God uses each of those conversations to walk me deeper into His truth. You know that I love you. I hope we live on the same street in the new earth . . . you know, that street where they put all the dancing people.

Thank you to Jerry and Carlye Arnold for loving me for almost twenty years. Thank you for keeping my room ready for me to crash. Thank you for introducing me to the finest Mexican food known to mankind, but more importantly you have introduced me to the beautiful freedom of Christ. Nobody can dance like you. I love you, love you, love you.

Thank you, Nicole, for a gracious no-matter-what-comes and no-matter-how-far friendship.

Maybe the people who carry me the most are my mom and dad, Joe and Novie Thomas. Thank you for every time you help me with the children, every meal you make and put in my freezer, every thoughtful phone call to see if I landed. And all the times you keep believing in me beyond reason. There are no words for this kind of lavish love. I love you and ask God to multiply back to you His blessings.

My deepest delight comes from my children, Grayson, William, Taylor, and AnnaGrace. Thanks for the stories you let me share so that someone else can grow. Thank you for brushing my hair when I'm tired. Thank you for the purest love I have ever known. Being your mom is the best thing ever.

Above all these is my Savior, Jesus. Every good gift is from Your hand and I know full well each of these gifts has been given to me by You. Please take these words, shape them as You wish, and use them for Your glory. I love You and I will serve You with gratefulness forever.

notes

Introduction

1. Encarta® *World English Dictionary* © 1999 Microsoft Corporation. All rights reserved. Developed for Microsoft by Bloomsbury Publishing Plc.

2. *The American Heritage*® Dictionary of the English Language, Fourth Edition (Boston: Houghton Mifflin Company, 2000).

Chapter 1

1. Henri J. M. Nouwen, *The Return of the Prodigal Son* (New York: Image Books, Doubleday, 1994), 12.

Chapter 2

1. Nouwen, *The Return of the Prodigal Son*, 16.

2. Ibid., 82.

3. James G. Friesen et al., *The Life Model: Living from the Heart Jesus Gave You* (Van Nuys: Shepherd's House, 2000), 7.

4. Gordon MacDonald, *Restoring Your Spiritual Passion* (Nashville: Oliver Nelson, 1986), 26.

5. Ibid., 34.

6. Friesen, *The Life Model*, 16.

7. Philip Yancey, *What's So Amazing About Grace?* (Grand Rapids, MI: Zondervan, 1997), 11.

Chapter 3

1. Oswald Chambers, *My Utmost for His Highest*, Classic Edition (Uhrichsville: Barbour, 1935), October 8 devotional reading.

Chapter 4

1. John Ortberg, *The Life You've Always Wanted* (Grand Rapids, MI: Zondervan, 2002), 137.

2. Friesen, *The Life Model*, 8 (emphasis mine).

Chapter 5

1. Steve Brown, *When Your Rope Breaks* (Grand Rapids, MI: Baker, 1996), 79.

Chapter 6

1. Chambers, *My Utmost for His Highest*, August 1 devotional reading.

2. John Piper, *When I Don't Desire God: How to Fight for Joy* (Wheaton: Crossway Books, 2004), 42.

3. Chambers, *My Utmost for His Highest*, August 1 devotional reading.

4. Andrew Murray, *Abide in Christ* (New Kensington: Whitaker House, 1979), 23–24.

5. Brennan Manning, *Ruthless Trust* (San Francisco: Harper, 2000), 5–6.

6. Andrew Murray, *The Believer's Absolute Surrender* (Grand Rapids: Bethany House, 1985), 20.

Chapter 7

1. Chambers, *My Utmost for His Highest*, February 8 devotional reading.

2. Brennan Manning, *The Ragamuffin Gospel* (Sisters, OR: Multnomah, 2000), 14–15.

Chapter 8

1. Friesen, *The Life Model*, 6.

2. Charles Stanley, *The Wonderful, Spirit-filled Life* (Nashville: Thomas Nelson, 1992), 116.

3. Charles C. Ryrie, *The Holy Spirit* (Chicago: Moody Press, 1965), 94.

4. Ibid., 93.

Chapter 9

1. Friesen, *The Life Model*, 6.

2. http://abcnews.go.com/US/wireStory?id=315976.

3. Nouwen, *The Return of the Prodigal Son*, 18.

Chapter 10

1. Chambers, *My Utmost for His Highest*, December 24 devotional reading.

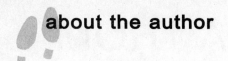

about the author

ANGELA THOMAS is a mother of four, dynamic speaker, and author of ten books and Bible studies including the best-selling book, *Do You Think I'm Beautiful?* Speaking from her own brokenness and God's great love, Angela motivates us all to live faithful, passionate lives. She teaches at numerous events every year where women all around the world are drawn to her warmth, wit, and vulnerability. Angela and her children live on a really great street in Knoxville, Tennessee, close to family and surrounded by some of the best people on the planet.

For more information on Angela, visit
www.angelathomas.com

For information on having Angela speak to your group, please contact:
Creative Trust
(615)297-5010
ATbooking@creativetrust.com